MASTERY OVER ANGER

Healing Relationships Through
Constructive Conflict-Resolution

I0161306

Sixth. Edition

James V. Potter, Ph.D. & Paula M. Potter, MA
© 2009 Jubilee Enterprises
ADVOCARE PUBLISHING CO.
Redding, California

MASTERY OVER ANGER:
HEALING   RELATIONSHIPS   THROUGH   CONSTRUCTIVE
CONFLICT-RESOLUTION, FIFTH EDITION

ISBN: 1930327501   EAN13: 9781930327504

Unless otherwise noted, all Biblical Scripture quotations in this volume are from the New International Version, Student Edition (NIV Study Bible),   Copyright © 1985 by the Zondervan Corporation, Grand Rapids, Michigan, U.S.A.

ISBN: 1930327501   EAN13: 9781930327504 - 51995

Published by Advocare Publishing Co.
Redding, California, U.S.A.

Printed in the United States of America

INTRODUCTION

To comprehend the significance that anger plays in today's society, family and workplace, and the problem it represents, one need only do a web search on the word. During my most recent search in April, 2007,, I noted that there were over eighty-eight million, six hundred thousand (88,600.000) hits under the word anger!

There are sights on 'controlling anger,' 'releasing anger,' 'the upside of anger,' 'the downside of anger,' 'the cost of anger,' 'the psychological effects of anger,' the physical effects of anger,' etc., etc. The list includes literally thousands of anger-management programs, books, tapes, videos, etc. Some of these books and programs advocate the concept of controlling, or managing, anger. Others suggest that anger is bad and one should rise above. Still others champion the idea of using anger to keep anger at bay.

One thing is certain, unbridled anger can and does produce negative, destructive outcomes including: manipulation, abuse and violence. These outcomes have serious consequences that damage relationships, destroy property, harm spouses, children, coworkers, neighbors and friends.

Mastery Over Anger, introduces a Psychoeducational program designed to help individuals who struggle with anger gain mastery over it. It teaches the student to use it constructively: to heal and nurture, rather than harm and destroy, their relationships. The material covered in this volume, when practiced, not only helps stop violence and abuse, but aids in the healing of personhood, the reconciliation of relationships and, the restoration of families.

This course provides keys to changing problematic behavior patterns and negative attitudes, facilitates the development of positive societal values and norms concerning the family structure, as well as the roles and tasks of its individual members. This course is intended to be used: as a self-study guide, as a textbook in counselor/facilitator training, and in facilitator-directed educational classes that are designed to impart family living skills to individuals, couples and families.

Mastery Over Anger, together with other volumes in the "Save Our Families" series, authored by Dr. James V. Potter, have been used as the curriculum in a number of court approved

Psychoeducational anger-management, domestic violence abatement, and batterer's intervention treatment programs.

The course is didactically (or educationally) focused and behavior-modification oriented, incorporating skill-streaming exercises designed to impart new living skills to the student.

It has been used with success by individuals who:

- Recognize they have problems managing their anger and desire to change,
- Have experienced violence and/or abuse of any kind in a boyfriend/girlfriend or spousal relationship,
- Have been the perpetrator in an assault and battery case against another person or persons,
- Have been the victim of family violence or assault and battery, or
- Have difficulty controlling their emotions and impulses, often reacting in anger or rage.

The primary objective in the design of the lessons in *Mastery Over Anger* is to help individuals struggling with anger and those counseling them. The goals of the course are to effect an immediate and complete cessation of family abuse, violence and other destructive life-controlling problems; to progressively reduce all forms of relationship abuse; and to help facilitate one's own personhood wholeness.

To accomplish these objectives, this skill-building program draws on aspects from several therapeutic approaches including, pastoral counseling, social-learning, cognitive therapy and behavioral therapy. Unlike many other anger-management program models that use a high level of confrontational intervention, this course is psychoeducationally focused. It provides a comparison between past pathological behavior patterns and more functional norms, providing students the specific skills needed to embrace these new behaviors.

Success in this program requires that students accept personal responsibility for their individual behavior, attitudes and beliefs; that they make a sincere commitment to embrace change; and that they consistently practice the new skills imparted. The course content helps students accomplish this by raising their awareness of the origins and nature of uncontrolled anger, family abuse and violence. Students learn to get in touch with, and interpret their emotions, gaining an understanding of the differences between emotional arousal and anger.

Course exercises teach students how to express themselves appropriately to others through dialogue and active listening, forgiveness and, in an understandable, non-confrontational manner, through psychodrama, role-playing, role-reversal and other practice assignments. Through this combined approach, students are able to gain an almost immediate improvement in their impulse-control and problem-solving abilities.

The earliest treatment programs for domestic violence and spousal abuse were generally provided by well-meaning clergy and counselors who were often inadequately trained and misinformed concerning the nature of anger and the dynamics of violence and abuse. As a result, they usually recommended the outdated, stereotypical solution that wives "submit" to their husbands and that husbands "protect" their wives.

When this attempt to mitigate the power and control issues within families failed, society's next attempt was to adopt a model of treatment committed to the task of separating the spouses, "rescuing" wives and girlfriends through the use of shelters, and punishing the husbands and boyfriends through incarceration and stay-away orders.

Treatment for wives and girlfriends (termed victims) and husbands and boyfriends (termed perpetrators or batterers) was provided totally in gender-specific classes with an implicit goal of helping the "victim" make an immediate and permanent separation from the "perpetrator."

That treatment modality, which is, unfortunately, still over-utilized today, is based on assumptions that men are nearly always the perpetrators and that women in abusive relationships desire to end the relationship and effect a separation or divorce to stop the abuse and violence. These assumptions have shaped, and continue to shape, policy, law and treatment protocol in our society, in spite of growing evidence that the underlying assumptions are incorrect.

Sound research indicates that *most* women and men who seek assistance for relationship violence and/or abuse would prefer to maintain the relationship, *if only* the violence could be eliminated (Geller, 1978). *Most* women who take advantage of shelters are seeking only a temporary refuge and plan to return to their husband or boyfriend after a brief stay (Walker, 1979; LaBell, 1979).

Nearly eighty-five percent (85%) of those women who report their husband, or boyfriend, for abusive, violent behavior later go to court and, either declaring the incident didn't happen the way they reported it, or to ask the court for clemency for the person they love.

The disparity between treatment goals and the victim's perceived need and desire for help has contributed to a growing cynicism among many professional providers (Pfouts, 1978). It has also generated a "get-tough" policy among lawmakers and enforcement agencies, without effecting any significant reduction in the incidence of domestic violence or the recidivism rate for offenders who have received treatment.

The majority of treatment programs that have attempted to interrupt or terminate the spousal relationship seem to have adopted a gender-specific view of spousal abuse and family violence. In their world view, males are seen as the unilateral source of violence and abuse and females as the defenseless victim. This view has served to polarize society, family members, many counselors and therapists and others who have experienced or been affected by family or relationship abuse or violence.

Unfortunately, this male/batterer and female/victim mentality has resulted in spouses, fiancees, siblings and coworkers viewing each other as enemies instead of helping all gain a more realistic perspective in which relationship dynamics, personality issues, external influences, life stresses, and interpersonal histories are correctly understood to be the sources of dysfunctional and inappropriate behavior.

Males have long been presumed to be the source of violence, either because of deep individual pathologies such as sociopathic or antisocial disorders, poor impulse-control, or authoritarian and patriarchal attitudes; or simply because they have experienced and internalized certain societal norms that tend to perpetuate violence (Dobash & Dobash, 1979; Martin, 1976; Pagelow, 1981; Walker, 1979).

More recent research, however, indicates that stress levels and marital adjustment issues, particularly issues of consensus, satisfaction, structure and cohesion, are more accurate predictors of domestic violence or the lack thereof (Neidig & Friedman, 1984; Olson, 1987).

When reported physical injuries are focused on as the primary concern, family violence is viewed as the harm that men do to women (Berk, Berk, Loske & Rauma, 1983). However, research efforts aimed at attempting to quantify various types of violent behavior practiced during conflicts between spouses have observed that "wives maintain their rough equality with respect to violence, irrespective of whether one measures it by incidence rate, mutuality of violence, degree of severity of the violent act, or prevalence of violence at each level of severity (Strass, 1980; Neidig & Friedman, 1984)."

While there may be compelling historical and political justification for maintaining the "male-batterer" view of spouse abuse, research indicates that personality disorders, poor family-of-origin training, and the resulting internalization of these poor family skills as "societal norms" are hardly gender-selective.

It is essential to remember that within the context of an ongoing relationship, the behavior of each individual is both contingent on, and influenced by, that of the other person. The behavior of each person can, in reality, be conceptualized as both a cause and an effect, depending on how the sequence of interactions progresses (Neidig & Friedman, 1984).

The interpersonal dynamics perspective of family abuse facilitates the development of personal responsibility and contributes to positive outcomes with appropriate intervention. In contrast to this, the unilateral responsibility perspective, with its emphasis on male perpetrators, female victims, and their family origins as the causative factor, tends to reduce guilt, decrease one's willingness to take personal responsibility, and increase a mutual sense of helplessness and hopelessness.

Finally, the unilateral responsibility perspective tends to result in fixed "perpetrator" and "victim" roles. Once assumed, these roles contribute to a more resistant perpetrator (who sees himself as the masculine "norm") and a helplessly contrite female (who believes she is the victim), both assuming that they have a legitimate right to vindictive punishment or other forms of retribution. These role assignments have been shown to contribute to ongoing violence which, over time, increases in frequency and escalates in lethality.

There is an old proverb that says, "Knowledge is power," and the knowledge gained through the *Mastery Over Anger* Psychoeducational skill-building program gives dedicated individuals the tools and the power to change. Those who complete the training exercises contained in this course, and practice the skills imparted, do change; and, as they change, the families to which they belong begin to change as well.

Family systems function much like an organic organism, in that when one component changes, it affects change throughout the whole organism. Couples and families whose individual members each apply themselves to acquire the same new skills, experience accelerated change. However, when even one person changes, it will effect change throughout his or her entire family, or organization, as a result of their ongoing transformation.

CONTENTS

CHAPTER 1
WHEN ANGER TURNS TO VIOLENCE

Overview:
To introduce the relationship between anger and violence, it seems appropriate to look at a few Scriptural admonitions concerning anger and its propensity toward violence. Consider, for example, the admonition of Moses, which describes the impact of man's uncontrolled anger:

"*Cursed be their anger, so fierce, and their fury, so cruel!* (Gen 49:7). *Or, the words of King David, who advised: "Refrain from anger and turn from wrath; do not fret — it leads only to evil"* (Ps 37:8); *"In your anger do not sin; when you are on your bed, search your heart and be silent"* (Ps 4:4).

King Solomon, ascribed as being the wisest person who has ever lived, said: "*A fool gives full vent to his anger, but a wise man keeps himself under control*" (Pr 29:11); "*An angry man stirs up dissension, and a hot-tempered one commits many sins*" (Pr 29:22). Solomon's words recorded in Ecclesiastes accurately predict the outcome of uncontrolled anger: "*Do not be quickly provoked in your spirit, for anger resides in the lap of fools*" (Eccl 7:9).

The apostle Paul advises that we "*Get rid of all bitterness, rage and anger, brawling and slander, along with every form of malice*" (Eph 4:31); and counsels, "*But now you must rid yourselves of all such things as these: anger, rage, malice, slander, and filthy language from your lips*" (Col 3:8). James, the brother of Jesus Christ advised: "*My dear brothers, take note of this: Everyone should be quick to listen, slow to speak and slow to become angry, for man's anger does not bring about the righteous life that God desires*" (Jas 1:19-20 NIV).

What is it about *man's* anger that leads to unrighteousness; that often escalates to acts of relationship abuse and violence? Anger is more than an emotion, it is a motivation to correct injustice and deal with impending danger. Anger is part of mankind's natural "fight or flight" instinct used in prehistoric times to respond to fearful and/or dangerous situations.

Humans often exhibit anger empathetically: for example, engaging in a civic action organization after reading an article about a minority experiencing racism or someone suffering from police brutality. We were not the victim, per se, but we feel the injustice. Thus, anger can be used to help us see what's wrong and motivate us to take action to correct the problem. In this case, our feelings, or emotions, are actually serving like intelligence agents, bringing us news from the field of our experience. We should not dismiss, ignore, or repress them; for righteous anger can help drive one to compassionate action, designed to redress the injustices in the world.

Every person has some anger within. Intense, angry feelings are not always unhealthy or destructive; nor do they necessarily drive negative actions. Anger is usually magnified and the duration of the experience extended during those times when a cognitive decision is made about the intent of the individual, organization or object, considered the cause of our concern or pain. In other words, if we decide that the injustice and resulting pain/deprivation were intentional or "deliberate," our emotions are usually intensified.

When anger is used in a way to "suppress opposition" though manipulation, emotional abuse, bullying or violence, the "bullier" and the "bullied" (the perpetrator and victim) often fail to realize that the root of anger is fear. The "angrier" and more "enraged" an individual appears to become, the more likely it is that that individual is experiencing increasingly greater fear.

Human emotions, including the feeling of fear, have their origin within two almond-shaped structures in the brain, called the amygdala. The amygdala is that part of the brain responsible for identifying threats, and for sending out an alarm when such threats are identified. The amygdala is so efficient at warning us about threats, that it often motivates us to react before the cortex (that part of the brain responsible for thought and judgment) has time to evaluate the appropriateness of our reaction. In other words, the brain is wired in such a way as to influence action before its consequences are logically considered.

As one's anger intensifies, their body's muscles tense up. Inside the brain, neurotransmitter chemicals known as catecholamines are released causing one to experience of a burst of energy that can last for some time. At the same time, the heart rate increases, the blood pressure rises, as does one's rate of breathing. Our face may flush as increased blood flow enters our limbs and extremities in preparation for quick physical action. In rapid succession, additional brain neurotransmitters and hormones, including adrenaline, noradrenaline and cortosol are released which trigger a lasting state of intense arousal.

These natural body chemicals help one deal with crises and solve problems. In prehistoric times, they enabled early man to ready himself for "flight or fight." This enabled man to run from a "saber-toothed tiger", or when cornered, turn and fight. It also served to help man meet other lesser threats. In these prehistoric times of crises, the elevated levels of stress hormones were burned up, or expended, during man's response to the impending emergency.

The world we now live in has changed significantly since that time, varying much faster than our instincts, motivations and/or our body chemistry. The situations we face in today's society are normally fairly trivial compared to those in prehistoric times, yet our body still responds to crises with massive outpourings of cortosol and adrenaline. If we haven't trained ourselves to resist overreacting to these daily situations, we place ourselves and our loved ones at risk: "a hair-trigger away from personal disaster".

Most often the escalation of our emotions from fear to anger, to wrath, rage and fury stops before getting out of control. The prefrontal cortex of the brain has been trained to keep our reaction to our emotions in proper perspective and proportion. In the same way the amygdala handles emotion, the prefrontal cortex handles judgment. The left, or analytic, prefrontal cortex can switch off the emotions. It serves in an executive role to keep things under control. Getting control of the emotions fueling anger necessitates learning ways to help the prefrontal cortex gain the upper hand over the amygdala so that when angry, we have control over our reactions to our feelings.

Anger has both a physiological preparation phase during which the body's resources are mobilized for a fight, a release phase, and a wind-down phase. During this wind-down phase, the body starts to regain its normal resting state, when the target of the anger no longer presents an immediate threat. None the less, it is difficult to relax from a state of intense anger very quickly. The adrenaline-caused arousal, occurring during anger, lasts a very long time (many hours, sometimes days). During this time, the anger threshold is lower than usual, making it much easier for the person to get angry once again.

It takes a rather long time for the body to return to its normal resting state. During this slow cool-down period the angered person is much more susceptible to experience anger in response to even minor irritations or frustrations. To respond appropriately to these in modern society, we need to develop and practice the ability to calmly and logically examine situations, circumstances and events, and respond in a measured way to prevent a poorly understood situation from escalating into a tragedy for all concerned.

Personal Application:
Describe, in your own words, what you believe that domestic violence means and includes:

_____

_____

Violence Defined
Violence has historically been rather narrowly defined and understood as physical force of sufficient intensity to cause bodily harm. However, since violence usually begins with nonphysical, mild or moderate intrusion onto the rights of another and then escalates to the point of harm or injury, we will use a much broader definition in this course.

Violence, as defined in this course, is the exertion of any form of force sufficient in strength and/or duration to cause injury and/or abuse of another's personhood, whether physical, mental, emotional or spiritual.

Synonyms for violence include: fury, force, pitch, intensity, ferocity, severity, vehemence, fierceness, infringement, profanation, pressure, compulsion, coercion, constraint, duress, manipulation, intimidation restraint, discordance, and threats. Viewing acts and/or omissions of acts within the framework of these synonyms may in time yield the beginning of a broader, more comprehensive definition of this growing relational problem.

Personal Application:
Based on the definition of violence given earlier, have you personally perpetrated or suffered from domestic violence? _____

If so, please describe the event(s):

_____

_____

4

What do you believe to have been the cause?

_____

_____

What was the outcome?

_____

_____

The Two Major Categories of Abuse

Research in the field of family abuse and violence indicates that there are two major categories of relational violence, which have been labeled "instrumental violence" and "expressive violence." They are best understood as the two polar extremes (or opposites) on the violence continuum.

Family abuse and violence can, theoretically, be located at any point on this continuum and an individual's pattern of acting out may be located at any point between these two extremes. It is uncommon for the majority of an individual's behavior to be at either extreme; most will tend to fall somewhere along the continuum between the polar extremes.

Violence Continuum

```
0 - - - - - - - - - - - - 50 - - - - - - - - - - - - - - 100
State of calm      Expressive           Instrumental
```

Acts of instrumental violence include those that are most often dramatized in movies and television. These serve as the basis for most of our laws relating to domestic violence. However, current research indicates that approximately ninety to ninety-five percent of all family violence falls short of this type of behavior, lying within the definition of expressive violence. Instrumental violence is believed to represent only five to ten percent of relational violence.

Personal Application:

What are your thoughts and feelings about violence? Should violence be treated the same, regardless of the type? Or, should the type of violence a person tends to use make a difference in their treatment plan?

_____

_____

Research suggests that the more effective intervention and treatment methods are influenced far less by the historical frequency and severity of violence in a relationship than by the nature of that violence, i.e., whether it is expressive or instrumental. Individuals who engage primarily in expressive violence are good candidates for Psychoeducational programs that are highly didactic (educational and skill-building). Individuals who engage primarily in instrumental violence usually respond better to more intense, confrontational intervention.

As a prerequisite to treatment, those employing instrumental violence may need to be referred out for a psychological/ psychiatric assessment, evaluation and treatment recommendations.

Personal Application:
How would you describe "expressive" violence:

_____

_____

Expressive Violence

Expressive violence is that form of violence that emanates during periods of high emotional arousal. It is considered to be a function of, and an expressive outlet for, those emotions. Typically, expressive violence occurs within the context of a gradually escalating disagreement where the level of conflict exceeds one's level of constructive communication and conflict-resolution skills. Incidents of expressive violence usually have a well-defined etiology, or origin. Adequate reflection on the part of those involved usually enables the parties to identify antecedent situations or circumstances that led to the conflict and escalated to triggering the acting-out incident.

Personal Application:
Expressive violence has been termed, by some writers, "mutual combat." Do you agree? If not, what is your understanding of mutual combat?

_____

Expressive violence nearly always involves a certain degree of mutuality in that both parties participate in the abusive and violent behavior. But, while there may be a high degree of mutuality, there is rarely if ever a sense of equality in the acts of violence. That is to say, when violence erupts, there is nearly always a "primary aggressor," or one who initiated the incident.

Personal Application:
Who are those who engage in expressive violence most likely to blame for their acts of violence and why?

Both parties -- the alleged perpetrator and apparent victim -- generally feel victimized and see themselves as respondents, reacting to the other person's provocative, aggressive behavior. Both parties experience a genuine sense of injustice, emotional pain, and genuine remorse and guilt for having acted in a manner that was inconsistent with their established moral values and convictions.

Personal Application:
Having blamed one another for the incident, which party in expressive violence is more likely to experience sorrow and/or remorse?

As a result of their shared responsibility and guilt, both parties actually experience a genuine sorrow and remorse for their actions.

Personal Application:
What, generally follows an episode of expressive violence?

The shock at having violated their own relationship rules, and the resulting sorrow, remorse, and desire to effect restitution, usually moves the couple from the episode of violence into a period of calm, conciliatory interaction, known as the *honeymoon* period. During this period, individuals who use a high degree of expressive violence are readily open to appropriate intervention. They are generally willing to assume personal responsibility for their behavior, once their denial and projection have been dealt with. The motivation to change in expressive violence is high.

Personal Application:
What activities can be carried out during the honeymoon phase that can help save relationships -- and why would they best be carried out now?

This *honeymoon* period is critical. If the parties desire to stay together or plan to reunite in the future, personhood safety measures need to be addressed simultaneously with skill-building. If both parties rapidly acquire new skills in anger control, stress management, communication skills, and conflict-resolution, the prognosis for eliminating violence and abuse, while preserving the relationship, is good.

Personal Application:
What is most apt to happen if help is not sought?

_____

_____

If help is not sought out or skill-training is delayed; repeated episodes of violence over the same, or similar unresolved issues will occur. This will result in the episodes of violence becoming more frequent and more instrumental with each failed conflict-resolution attempt.

Instrumental Violence:

Personal Application:
What is your understanding of "instrumental violence" and how does it differ from expressive violence?

_____

_____

Instrumental violence is the deliberate and often premeditated, use of violence as an instrument or tool to influence, control, and/or punish another person. This type of violence lacks the mutuality aspects that are common in expressive violence. Instrumental violence is the violence commonly portrayed in movies and on television that results in, and is appropriately referred to as, spouse or partner battering.

Reported incidents of instrumental violence are more often incidents of violence inflicted by men against women. Thus, they are accurately referred to as "wife-battering." Instrumental violence is used to punish the spouse's behavior that was deemed unacceptable to the batterer, or to control the spouse in an effort to prevent such unacceptable or undesirable behavior.

Personal Application:
What thing, or things, are most likely to trigger instrumental violence?

In contrast to the dynamics involved in expressive violence, in instrumental violence, there are few if any, episode antecedents (events leading up to the crisis). Instrumental violence has no apparent cause and the escalation from mild displeasure to explosive violence is almost instantaneous rather than gradual, progressive and sequential.

Personal Application:
In instrumental violence the mutuality of action in expressive violence is replaced with clear roles referred to as what?

What contributes to this difference?

In relationships where instrumental violence dominates, there are two clear roles: that of the perpetrator or batterer, and the victim or victims. The use of violence has been incorporated into the perpetrator's value system and is viewed by him/her as the norm. The perpetrator, therefore, experiences no guilt, sorrow, or genuine remorse. Quite the contrary; the aggressor normally feels vindicated, justified and rewarded by his/her actions.

Personal Application:
Why, under such circumstances, doesn't the battered spouse, or victim just leave?

Whereas the perpetrator of instrumental violence feels justified, the victim experiences a sense of hopelessness, purposelessness, helplessness and meaninglessness. She/he gradually loses her/his own reality and identity, and even fears the loss of their abuser. Their identity has become thoroughly enmeshed with the batterer's, resulting in the "battered spouse" syndrome.

The woman's or man's emotional submission and behavioral compliance to the batterer result in the reinforcement of the perpetrator's belief that he/she is right and justified in the actions taken. He/she experiences no personal discomfort as a result of having been violent. In fact, they can, and will, justify his acts to all who will listen.

Personal Application:
What activities commonly take place during the honeymoon period in cases involving instrumental violence, and how do these differ from those in expressive violence?

_____

_____

The perpetrator may, having exhibited acts of violence, thereafter express his/her "sorrow" and "remorse" but, these will be shallow and non-genuine. To the untrained observer or inexperienced "helper" there may still appear to be a *honeymoon* period. In reality, this is a self-centered attempt by the perpetrator to whitewash the truth and exercise yet another form of control. By doing this, he/she is able to keep his/her spouse from telling, or leaving. By giving his/her spouse one of the few positive relational rewards that they ever receive: temporary kindness, they keep them dependent and trapped.

Personal Application:
What is the best method of intervening when instrumental violence dominates in a relationship?

_____

_____

The appropriate intervention strategy in cases where instrumental violence prevails involves immediate separation, the victim's referral to a refuge or shelter, most often the wife, and children if any. This should be accompanied by timely legal sanctions against the perpetrator. It must be recognized that the greater the evidence of instrumentality in family violence incidents, the greater the propensity of lethality. The more often that instrumental violence occurs in a relationship, the more extensive the level of sanctions required to protect the victim(s) and witnesses from further personal harm.

Personal Application:
What effect, if any, does the use of alcohol or other mood-altering substances have on domestic violence and why?

_____

_____

_____

Persons who are actively abusing drugs and/or alcohol, as well as those suffering from antisocial and sociopathic tendencies, are more likely to experience substantial cognitive distortions (thought process disorders). They also tend to have more limited coping skills. They will require more frequent, more intense, and usually more confrontational, intervention to address the high levels of denial, projection, isolation, rejection, and rescuer-seeking self-blame defenses.

Expressive and instrumental violence have a number of similarities. They both have the potential for resulting in psychological and physical harm. The manifestation of either will damage relationships and will, if timely intervention does not take place, increase in frequency and severity. As every episode of violence tends to be worse, there is an increased potential for lethality.

There are also some distinct differences between Expressive and Instrumental violence. These need to be recognized and properly addressed when selecting the most appropriate and effective treatment modality, interventions and perpetrator sanctions.

In order to provide appropriate intervention in cases of domestic violence, one must first have an understanding of the nature and scope of the problem. In developing this understanding, it is essential to separate research from rhetoric, fact from fiction, and pragmatic exactness from political correctness.

The domestic violence statistics promulgated during the past few years indicate that family abuse and violence is basically an issue of gender differences in power and control. Most media information available features male perpetrators and female victims. Typical statistical reports, published primarily by women advocacy groups recount the following:

- Nearly one-third of women will be abused by their intimate partner.

- Violence inflicted by an intimate partner accounts for approximately 21% of all violence suffered by women and only about 2% of all violence suffered by men.

- Roughly 92% of all domestic violence incidents involve crimes against women by men.

- Approximately 28% of all female homicide victims are killed by their male partners while just over 3% of males are killed by their female partners.

- Women are attacked six times more often than males in incidents of intimate violence.

Society has become so accustomed to hearing these and similar statistics, most accept them without taking time to question their validity or personally investigate the facts. To correct the problem, se must correctly understand the issue. To achieve this, it is essential that we momentarily set aside these familiar statistics and any preconceived ideas, and examine current research findings.

To aid in this endeavor, the following exerts are cited from recent research articles, reported in an annotated bibliography on the subject prepared by Martin S. Fiebert, Department of Psychology, California State University, Long Beach. The referenced bibliography examines 155 scholarly research articles; 126 empirical studies and 29 literature reviews or analyses. The aggregate sample size in the reviewed studies exceeds 116,000. For more details the reader is recommended to refer to the entire annotated bibliography @:
http://www.csulb.edu/mfiegert/assault.htm.

The following is a sampling of these referenced documents, illustrating the difference between documented fact and information generally made available to the public:

- A sample of actively dating college students including 204 females and 140 males, who responded to a survey examining courtship violence indicated that there were no significant differences between the genders in self-reported perpetration of violence in their relationships. *Aizenman, M., & Kelly, G. (1988).*

- Meta-analyses of gender differences in agressivity between heterosexual partners indicate that women are more likely than men to use acts of violence, and to use such acts in greater frequency. In terms of injuries sustained, women were more likely to suffer injuries, the analyses indicating that 62% of those who reported being injured were women. *Archer, J. (2000), Psychological Bulletin, 126, 651-680.*

- Analyzing responses to a "Conflict Tactics Scale, women were more likely than men to throw things at their partner, as well as to slap, kick, bite, punch and hit with objects, while men were more likely to strangle, choke or physically beat up their partners. *Archer, J. (2002).*

- Of those completing the Conflict Tactics Scale, women were significantly more likely than their male partners to express their violence physically. *Archer, J. & Ray, N. (1989), Aggressive Behavior, 15, 337-343.*

- Using the Conflict Tactics Scale with a sample of 270 undergraduates -- 95 men and 175 women -- researchers found that 30% of men and 49% of women reported using aggression during their dating history, with a greater percentage of women engaging in severe physical aggression. *Arias, I, Samios, M & O'Leary, K. D. (1987)*

- Another study employing this same scale, involving a sample of 103 males and 99 females, found that 19% of women and 18% of men admitted being physically aggressive with their partners. *Arias I, & Johnson P. (1989).*

- A study in "Violent Intimacy" surveying 461 college students, found that 15% of the men and 21% of the women acknowledged physically abusing their partners. *Bernard, M. L. & Bernard, J. L. (1983).*

- The Canadian Journal of Psychiatry (31, 129-137) reporting on a survey among 1,200 randomly selected Canadians, reported that women both initiated and engaged in violence at higher rates than their male partners. *Bland, R. & Orne, H. (1986).*

- While most violence in relationships appears to be mutual -- 36% reported by women and 38% by men -- women report initiating violence with their nonviolent male partners more frequently than men with their female partners (22% vs. 17%). *Bookwala, J., Frieze I. H., Smith, C. & Ryan K. (1992).*

- A community wide sample of at-risk young couples, employing the Conflict Tactics Scale, reported these gender comparisons: 9.4% of men and 13.2% of women perpetrated frequent acts of physical violence against their partner. And, contrary to what was expected, 13% of the men and 9% of the women indicated they had been physically injured at least once, while 2% of the men and none of the women indicated that they had been injured by their partner between five and nine times. *Capaldi, D. M. & Owen, L. D. (2001).*

- While most domestic violence literature being promulgated today portrays women as the "recipients of domestic violence -- epidemiological surveys on the distribution of violent behavior between adult partners suggest gender parity." *Coney, N. S. & Mackey, W. C. (1999).*

- Contrary to the frequently touted assertions that certain minority ethnicities practice more domestic violence than others, research indicates otherwise. A sample involving 1440 couples -- 565 white, 358 black and 527 Hispanic, indicates that the overall incidence of aggression and violence is similar for all ethnicities. In terms of gender, white men and women demonstrated a parity of partner aggression, while Hispanic women were more aggressive than their male partners, and black men were more aggressive than black women. *Cunradi, C. B., Caetano, R., Clark, C. L. & Schafer, J. (1999).*

- When domestic violence is not reciprocal, or mutual, men were three times more likely than women to report being victimized, and violence in past relationships was the best overall predictor of violence in current relationships. *Deal, J. E. & Wampler, K. S. (1986).*

- When one partner could be labeled as the usual initiator, or primary aggressor, of violence in a relationship, that partner is most frequently the woman -- regardless of race. *DeMaris, A, (1992).*

- One study found that women were more likely to act out aggressively in relationships than men because they don't believe their male partners will be injured or retaliate. Women also claim that they assault their male partners because they want their attention and involvement, particularly emotional. *Feibert, M. S., & Gonzales, D. M. (1997).*

- Gender differences are also evident in aggression motivation. In a broad base study, women were found to be twice as likely to report having perpetrated violence as men and women attribute their male partner's violence to a desire to gain control or retaliate for having been hit first. In contrast, most men believe that female aggression emanates from a female's desire to demonstrate just how angry they really are, thereby retaliating for feeling emotionally mistreated. *Follingstad, D. R.. Wright, S., & Sebastin, J. A. (1991).*

- One of the more renowned researchers in the research field, R. J. Gelles, laments the complete lack of objectivity on the part of the "feminists" concerning research demonstrating female perpetrated domestic violence. *Gelles, R. J. (1994).*

- A study of domestic violence in the United Kingdom found that the single highest at-risk group for being victimized in domestic violence incidents are single men, abused by their present partner, or former partners. *George, M. J. (1999).*

- A research project surveying adolescent dating violence found that mutual combat was present in 66% of the cases and when there was a clear perpetrator, or primary aggressor, 29% of the women and 4% of the men reported being the sole perpetrator, comparing with 8% of the women and 26% of the men who reported being the victim of intimate violence. *Gray, H. M., & Foshee, V. (1997).*

- The rate of severe violence of husbands against wives decreased 33% from 1975 to 1985, while the rate of severe violence of wives against husbands increased 42% during that same period. *Hampton, R. L., Gelles, R. J., & Harrop, J. W. (1989).*

- A reexamination of the data from the current National Violence Against Women survey (Tjaden & Thoennes, 1998) indicates that "assaulted men are more likely than assaulted women to experience serious attacks by being hit with an object, beat up, threatened with a knife or being knifed." *Hoff, B. H. (1999).*

- A study in the Journal of Family Violence reported that 25% of husbands and 11% of wives could be identified as being mildly aggressive while 53% of wives and 36% of husbands could be classified as being severely aggressive. Moreover, 68% of the couples surveyed, surveyed independently, were in agreement on the gender specificity of aggression in their relationship. *Langhinrichsen-Rohling, J., & Vivian, D. (1994).*

- An examination of domestic violence based on an analysis of official data and national victimization, as reported in the Justice Quarterly, 1, 171-193, reviewing 6,200 cases of spousal abuse in the Detroit Michigan area, found that men had used a weapon 25% of the time while female assailants used weapons 86% of the time. *McLeod, M. (1984).*

- A ten year study in the United States, culminating in 1989, found higher murder rates of wives than husbands -- 43.4% vs. 56.6%. Black husbands were at the greatest risk of victimization, and homicide rates among interracial marriages was 7.7 times higher. Husbands and wives were equally likely to be killed by firearms -- about 72% of the time -- while husbands were more likely to be stabbed while wives were more likely to be bludgeoned to death. *Mercy J. A. & Saltzman, L. E. (1989).*

- A broad based study conducted in six different countries, including the United States, found that in all societies, the percentage of husbands who used violence was similar to the percentage of violent wives. The major exception noted was that "wives who used violence ... tended to use greater amounts." *Stets, J. E. & Henderson, D. A. (1991).*

- Contrary to a popular notion about women's violence against men, researchers have concluded that the violence perpetrated by women is not primarily defensive in nature. *Stets, J. E. & Strass, M. A. (1990).*

- A feminist analysis of the problem, published in the Psychology of Women Quarterly, 18, 487-508, acknowledges that "women equal or exceed men in number of reported aggressive acts committed within the family." *White, J. W., & Kowalski, R. M. (1994).*

- Despite the popularly promulgated statistics on spousal homicide, an article published in Criminology, 30, 189-215, indicates that for every 100 men who kill their wives, about 75 wives killed their husbands. *Wilson, M. I. & Daley, M. (1992).* [With the current trend involving a reduction in the incidence of violent acts of men against women and a corresponding increase in the incidence of violent acts of women against men, the gender ratio in spousal homicide is nearly equal.]

- Children are also at risk and are frequently victims in family violence. The Heritage Foundation reports that an average of six (6) children die as a result of domestic violence each day. This equals nearly 2,000 per year. Moreover, a detailed analysis of the perpetrator in these child deaths is disturbing. The Heritage Foundation reports estimates that 1,100 of these children are killed by their mothers compared to only 137 by their biological father! Stepfathers account for an estimated 250 of these deaths and live-in boyfriends are responsible for 513. This means that nearly 81% of children killed in family violence incidents are killed by their own mothers and/or their mother's live-in boyfriend.

The purpose in providing this information is certainly not intended to indict women and exonerate men. Rather, it is provided to help uncover truth in hopes of improving society's response to domestic violence, and aid in the development of more effective therapeutic interventions. Hopefully, the citations provided above will help pierce the veil of political correctness that has been erected to shroud the truth: and clearly establish the fact that domestic violence is a human issue rather than a gender issue.

Research indicates that nearly 95% of all domestic violence is manifest as expressive violence, compared to only 5% being instrumental violence. That is to say that most violence is an aberrant, reactive expression of one's emotions rather than an intentional, instrumental responsive use of power and control to hurt, control and/or punish.

Associated with our misunderstanding of the problem, is society's inappropriate and ineffective response. The typical response has been to vilify the male and identify the female as the victim. This conceptualization of the problem has resulted in a typical scenario where the father and husband -- usually the primary income generator -- is removed from the home and incarcerated while the wife and mother is subjected to undue financial hardship and encouraged to participate in programs designed to foster a victim mentality in women.

This response contributes to undue stress resulting in the termination of one troubled relationship and the premature development of replacement relationships in an effort to help meet financial needs. The end result of this response to the problem is an alarming increase in child physical and sexual abuse and fatality.

There are numerous other outcomes generated by this mishandling of the problem, as indicated in the following statistics:

- 63% of all youth suicides are from fatherless homes (Bureau of the Census).

- 90% of all homeless and runaway children are from fatherless homes.

- 85% of all children that exhibit behavioral disorders come from fatherless homes (Center for Disease Control).

- 80% of rapists motivated by displaced anger come from fatherless homes (Criminal Justice & Behavior, Vol. 14. P. 403-416, 1978).

- 71% of all high school dropouts come from fatherless homes (National Principals Association Report on the State of High Schools).

- 75% of all adolescent patients in chemical abuse/dependency treatment centers come from fatherless homes (Rainbows for all God's Children).

- 70% of all juveniles in state-operated mental health institutions come from fatherless homes (US Department of Justice, special Report, Sept. 1988).

- 85% of all youths sitting in prisons grew up in a fatherless home (Fulton Co., Georgia - Jail Populations, Texas Department of Corrections, 1992).

- The majority of those who develop Borderline Personality Disorder, grew up in fatherless homes and were subject to severe abuse, most frequently by their natural mother and her boyfriends.

it also behooves us as a society all to be aware of other, serious and far reaching statistics:

- Peace Officers spend one-third (33-1/3%) of all their on-duty time responding to domestic violence calls.

- Sixty percent (60%) of all injuries incurred by police officers are received while responding to domestic violence calls.

- Forty percent (40%) of all police officers killed in the line of duty die while responding to a domestic violence incident.

- Domestic violence is the most underreported crime in America. It is estimated that less than five percent (5%) of domestic violence victims report incidents of domestic abuse and violence.

In recognition of the foregoing, indisputable facts, based on sound research, it is essential that our methodology and approach be amended if the problem of domestic violence is to be corrected in our society. Some of the adjustments needed are obvious:

- We must correct our thinking about gender participation and our subsequent identification of both perpetrator and victim.

- We must recognize that a great deal of domestic violence should be viewed within the context of "mutual combat" while recognizing that this does not infer that the combatants are equal in the harm inflicted or injury sustained.

- We must, in light of research supporting the high level of mutuality in domestic violence, recognize that all parties involved in incidents of violence need therapeutic intervention to alter their relationship dynamics.

- We need to undertake major revisions in our therapeutic approach to the problem to insure that all parties learn new skill sets to prevent the multigenerational transmission of this problem.

- We must, as a society, invest more resources into treating the troubled family, doing whatever is possible to preserve the integrity of the family unit, rather than proliferate domestic violence and manifold associated problems by disrupting the family unit.

- We need to recognize that by disrupting family units rather than providing appropriate treatment for all parties, we encourage dysfunctional individual family members to develop new dysfunctional relationships. giving rise to more incidents of violence.

- We need to recognize the difference in dynamics between expressive violence and instrumental violence which require variations in therapeutic interventions, and legal sanctions.

The more effective approach for instrumental violence is long-term gender-specific group therapy. Effective therapeutic interventions are those that are directive, confrontational and intense enough to break through the perpetrator's denial and challenge their aberrant value systems. Those who dominate in the use of instrumental violence need to be evaluated for mental health and personality disorders. When determined to be present, the person's treatment plan needs to supplemented with individual psychotherapy and appropriate psychotropic medication.

Persons exhibiting primarily instrumental violence normally require more stringent legal sanctions that may include, long-term incarceration, temporary or permanent stay-away orders to protect the victim(s); the imposition of significant fines and court ordered restitution of amounts sufficient to help them understand the seriousness and unacceptability of their actions. When placed on probation or parole, these persons require longer probation/parole terms with significant to intense supervision. These individuals are far more likely than those employing expressive violence to re-offend and far less likely to complete court mandated treatment, or fulfill court/probation conditions.

Individuals who exhibit violence that is primarily expressive in nature, respond best to a treatment plan that commences with gender-specific group therapy and, at the appropriate time, includes couples and even family therapy. Intervention techniques that are most effective with persons who manifest expressive violence are those that are Psychoeducational and skill-building in nature since the primary factor contributing to expressive violence is the lack of adequate relational skills (i.e., communication, conflict-resolution, time and financial management, etc.,), rather than the more aberrant antisocial ideations of those manifesting primarily instrumental violence.

Persons whose pattern of violence is primarily expressive in nature, usually benefit from a temporary separation, temporary restraining order, and when appropriate, short-term incarceration. Since these persons are more motivated toward, and amenable to, change, techniques such as brief intermittent incarcerations for re-offenses and/or threats usually serve to rapidly diminish their acting out and materially decrease their recidivism rates.

GLOSSARY

Antecedent (p. 5) -- Prior, previous events, earlier things that have led up to the event.

Conciliatory (p. 5) -- Designed to console or comfort.

Denial (p. 5) -- As used here, psychological denial, or one's inability or unwillingness to look at negative and/or unpleasant matters.

Didactic (p. 5) -- Teaching, or skill-transfer focused.

Emanates (p. 5) -- Originates, or comes from, as the source of origin.

Enmeshed (p. 6). -- Entangled, confused with.

Etiology (p. 5) -- Origin.

Expressive Violence (p. 5, etc.) -- Violence that erupts as a function of expression when one's stress increases and communication and conflict-resolution skills are deficient.

Instrumental Violence (p. 5, etc.) -- Violence used with intent as a instrument, or weapon, to inflict harm, punishment, or to maintain dominance over another.

Prognosis (p. 6) -- Outlook or forecast.

Projection (p. 5) -- As used here, psychological projection, when one projects their thoughts, feelings and/or action on another (e.g., as though coming from a projector), causing them to believe the other person is the source.

Provocative (p. 5) -- Intended to provoke another person to action.

Sequential (p. 6) -- Consecutive, a series of events.

Violence (p. 5, etc.) -- The exertion (or use) of any form of force of sufficient strength or duration (length of time) to cause injury, or fear of injury to another's personhood.

KEY POINTS

- **Categories of Violence:**
  - Expressive
  - Instrumental
- **Differences between categories:**

- **Preferred Treatment plan:**

- **Appropriate Legal Sanctions:** (Review summary)

CHAPTER 2
The Cycle of Violence

If I have heard it said once, I've heard it a thousand times, "This is the first time anything like this has happened. I've never been violent before and I will never do it again." Only a very naive person or codependent spouse will believe that line. Violence is not a rare, isolated, random event in the life of an otherwise healthy, happy relationship. Quite the contrary, violence in a relationship, whether expressive or instrumental, nearly always begins with nonphysical forms of abuse and escalates to the incident that finally demands an intervention of some nature.

There is a very predictable, sequential pattern that individuals and couples can learn to recognize and use to help prevent violence and control the frequency and intensity of their conflicts. The keys to initiating conflict control include having an understanding of the sequence and early recognition of the signals that the conflict is escalating. Once mastered, this understanding and signal recognition become tools for conflict containment and emotional de-escalation.

Lenore Walker (1979) identified a three-phase cycle of violence model that is still used in most domestic violence literature today. The three phases are:

- The tension-building phase
- The explosion or violent episode
- The honeymoon period or remorse phase

Although Lenore Walker's research and formulations were based primarily on the behaviors noted in instrumental violence, normally termed, battering relationships, her model nonetheless is applicable to some extent in all relationships experiencing violence and abuse. The cyclic phases may vary in length between the two forms of violence and may not be as detectable in the early stages of expressive violence as in instrumental violence. None the less, her work does provide a conceptual framework for understanding abusive and violent behavior. Walker's three-phase model is depicted below.

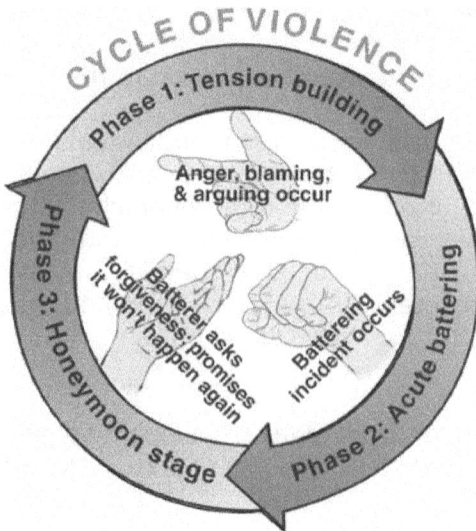

CYCLE OF VIOLENCE

Phase 1: Tension building

Anger, blaming, & arguing occur

Batterer asks forgiveness, promises it won't happen again

Battereing incident occurs

Phase 3: Honeymoon stage

Phase 2: Acute battering

Phase One:
Tension-Building Phase
Personal Application:
Based on your personal experience or understanding, what most frequently triggers the tension-building phase in a conflict?

_____

_____

_____

_____

_____

_____

Phase one, the tension-building phase, can be triggered by nearly any unresolved issue that creates tension or stress, including the most recent episode of violence or release. Even the antecedent honeymoon period can trigger the tension-building phase as one or both parties begin to wonder how long *this* honeymoon period will last, and conjecture when the next episodic release of violence will occur.

The trigger may be verbal -- the words the other person speaks, the inflection they use (volume, pitch, speed, pressure, clarity, etc.), or it may be body language -- the other's physical behavior, including looks, hand signals, gestures, posture, etc. The trigger is often a seemingly unrelated event or circumstance such as a spouse or child coming home intoxicated, the receipt of a disturbing telephone call, or a review of the monthly bills and the realization that there are insufficient funds to meet the obligations.

Personal Application:
What is one of the more common defense mechanisms often employed in an attempt to avoid arguments that can actually trigger the tension- building phase?

_____

_____

A common trigger for initiating the tension-building phase is one party withdrawing and/or isolating themselves from the other, causing the other person to experience a sense of rejection and/or abandonment. For example: a man believes that he cannot keep up with his partner's verbal communication (since most women think faster, speak faster, have a longer attention span, and involve more emotional content in their speech). In "self-defense" he may attempt to tell his partner that he is becoming overwhelmed but, in frustration, he often expresses himself by demanding that she "back-off," "shut-up," or "bug-out."

The wife, in turn, may interpret her partner's demands as evidence that he doesn't care or isn't interested in her thoughts, feelings, or concerns. Depending on her own woundedness, the wife may withdraw with hurt feelings. However, it is more likely, based on current research, that she will increase her efforts to reach him by speaking more loudly, crying, calling names and even blocking his retreat if he attempts to leave.

Whichever course she takes at this point, the man is likely to feel abandoned and rejected, and retaliate by initiating counter-rejection against her. This pattern of circular feedback fuels misinterpretation and misunderstanding usually resulting in escalating emotions that often mount to the point of triggering another incident of violence.

Phase Two - The Release or Violent Episode

Personal Application:
Based on your personal experience or exposure, how long, comparatively, do the tension-building and the release phase, resulting in acts of violence usually last?

_____

_____

Phase one may last anywhere from a few minutes to a period of days, weeks or months. Relationships that involve primarily expressive violence usually experience fairly long periods of tension-building during the early part of their relationship, periods that tend to grow shorter and shorter with each cycle. In contrast, those relationships that involve primarily instrumental violence usually experience very, very short tension-building cycles.

Typically, phase one results in mounting levels of tension which, after reaching an intolerable level, are explosively discharged through one or more methods of violent expression as phase two begins. The duration of phase two is usually very short in the early stages of expressive violence, but much longer in relationships experiencing instrumental violence, sometimes lasting days.

These differences are primarily due to the fact that expressively violent individuals are acting against their basic values, while the instrumentally violent persons are acting in a manner than coincides with their basic beliefs and value systems.

Personal Application:
Can expressive violence turn into instrumental violence? _____

If so, what is the most common cause?

_____

The differences between expressive and instrumental violence begin to diminish with recurrent episodes of expressive violence. Cycle by cycle, As the parties' values begin to change to accommodate the abuse, the nature of the violence changes. Imperceptibly it moves from the expressive type toward the instrumental type of violence. As it does, the tension-building phase becomes shorter and shorter, the episodes of violence longer and longer, and the honeymoon phase becoming less genuine and more designed to justify, to cover up the perpetrator's acts of violence.

Personal Application:
What, if any are the differences between men's and women's communication styles, and do these have any bearing on domestic violence?

_____

_____

_____

28

One of the factors affecting both the tension-building and release phase is the gender difference in communication styles. Men and women communicate quite differently. Women are much more relationship oriented. Nearly 100% of all verbal sounds they make are "intelligible" communication, or conversation. Their conversation is laden with much more emotional content than the average male's, and their attention span is approximately three times longer than most men's.

Men, in comparison, incorporate a significant amount of sound in their communication -- sound that not comprised of words, as such, but appearing to be just noise. These seemingly non-intelligible sounds comprise as much as forty percent (40%) of male communication according to some researchers. And, these "unintelligible" sounds are not just meaningless noise. They form of system, or method, of communication.

Men often feel overwhelmed by the emotional content of their partner's apparent circular reasoning. If asked for their feelings men often feel that they are being interrogated or that their integrity is being questioned. Most women have little, if any, knowledge of the masculine form of verbal but seemingly non-intelligible, communication. Not understanding this form of communication, most women view these sounds, designed to provide clues to the man's emotional state, unintelligible as put-downs, intimidation, and threats.

There is research-based speculation that male children develop symbolized, non-word verbal signals that are well understood by other male children. These non-word sounds are verbalized symbols, researchers contend, that clearly convey between male children, when they are about to attack one another or when they are ready to give up and retreat. These signals, it is believed, serve to ward off, or terminate, most incidents of violence between male children. Females, who are not socialized in this manner, usually have not developed the ability to recognize these non-word sounds as signals, or if recognized, fail to understand them (Neidig & Friedman, 1984).

Personal Application:
It has been alleged that men are just naturally more aggressive. Do you believe this to be true, and if so what evidence of this is there?

_____

A male child's acculturalization often seems to include an implicit understanding that certain things "demand" a physical response to preserve their dignity, identity and self-worth. Few females seem to carry this same intrinsic belief and therefore rarely understand what the man is attempting to establish when he responds physically or in unintelligible sounds. These divergent acculturated norms often result in both parties (husbands and wives) feeling misunderstood and victimized.

Personal Application:
If these differences exist, what can one do to "balance the accounts?"

Learning to communicate in an honest, open manner that turns implicit concepts into explicit expectations and desires has tremendous potential for reducing triggering mechanisms in the cycle of violence. The greater the clarity in a couple's communication, the better the understanding one another's communicative styles. The sooner they recognize anger cues and each other's trigger mechanisms, the easier it becomes to avert emotional escalation and resulting episodes of violence.

Couples who know little about one another's intrinsic beliefs, values and implicit expectations usually fail to realize the signs of escalation. By the time they recognize these symbols and comprehend the probability of escalation, the situation may have already become violent. At this point, it is usually too late to prevent the incident.

Phase Three - The Honeymoon Period

Personal Application:
What activities commonly take place during the "honeymoon period?"

The nervous tension that built up during phase one has been dissipated during the explosive release of tension (the episode of violence) during phase two. This introduces a period of relative serenity and calm usually referred to as the honeymoon period. Apologies, expressions of forgiveness,

extension of physical affection, and promises that "it will never happen again" are common.

The primary aggressor, or more violent partner, often resorts to giving gifts while the more victimized party often resorts to conciliatory gestures that affirm the relationship and the other person's value. For example, the husband who has recently abused his wife, may go out and buy her flowers, candy, a new blouse, etc. to demonstrate his love. While he is gone, his wife may fix him his favorite meal, put on his favorite dress, or prepare herself to be more appealing on his return, to demonstrate that she still loves and cares for him.

Personal Application:
How sincere are these acts of restitution and kindness?

In expressive violence the sorrow and remorse exhibited are genuine since the parties have acted against their established values. Their apologies, forgiveness, affection and self-blame are real. Their fear of losing the one they love and their promises for making behavioral change are sincere. Unfortunately, the deck is stacked against them unless they get professional help.

Personal Application:
If the parties are so sincere and willing to make amends, why are they so likely to repeat the destructive behavior?

Couples who are committed to one another, usually interact in the best way they know how, within the skill level they have. Unless they get help to increase their relationship skills, they are destined to repeat the cycle of violence. Moreover, most have been frequently rewarded exhibiting violence -- the wife with gifts and the husband with affection and his favorite meal! They have learned through this symbolized subconscious learning, that the route to gifts and affection is through the release of tension in a violent manner. This is termed, "operant conditioning" an expression used to explain the enforcement effects of rewards and punishments.

By trying to appease one another and express their remorse and love through rewards, the expressively violent couple is thus being conditioned to continue their violent relationship patterns. Of even greater concern, with each episode of violence, each incident of broken promises, the violence in this relationship moves imperceptibly from expressive toward instrumental violence.

Personal Application:
How does the honeymoon period differ when instrumental violence dominates?

_____

In relationships where instrumental violence prevails there is also a honeymoon period; however, the dynamics and implicit expectations supporting it are very different. The perpetrator, having battered his/her partner into submission, has lost their sense of fear that their partner may leave him and is now primarily concerned that they may tell -- their children, the police, their pastor, doctor, etc.

Personal Application:
What does the perpetrator's fear often drive him/her to do, and why?

_____

_____

The perpetrator's fear of exposure and punishment usually drives him/her to feign remorse and give their victim gifts or favors to buy "protection." They experience no genuine remorse, for by now the perpetrator's belief systems and values have been modified to regard their violent behavior as normal, appropriate and necessary to maintain "order and control" in the family. The victim's gestures of affection and/or service are no longer expressions of love. Instead, they are gestures made in stark fear -- fear for their own and their children's lives.

The victim of instrumental violence experiences a growing sense of helplessness and despair, depression and meaninglessness. They often stay in the relationship which mystifies onlookers, but they stay because they have become so depersonalized, made so dependent on the perpetrator, that they genuinely believe that there is no way out -- that they could not possibly survive without him/her. Beyond this, most victims have been convinced -- by the perpetrator -- that they are of such little value, no one else would even want them. They have over time convinced them that they are doing them a favor by allowing them to stay!

Personal Application:
If the victim becomes so hopeless and helpless, why do such a high number of battered spouses kill, or attempt to kill, their partners?

During the honeymoon period in instrumental violence, there is another very sickening aspect of the cycle of violence that sends subtle messages of hope to even the most battered spouse. The level of intimacy experienced during this phase of the cycle, usually exceeds that of any other time. The perpetrator's expressions of remorse, although feigned, may involve increased transparency and disclosure of personal vulnerability and weakness that would otherwise remain concealed. As the perpetrator shares these weaknesses and admits their need for help, there is often a sudden shift in power and control. The victimized partner now feels that they are the stronger of the two and therefore responsible to protect and nurture the perpetrator.

There is an old parable seems to apply here: "He who has the least to lose has the greatest power." It is fairly common in abusive relationships that the person who has been abused, who called 911 for emergency response or threatened to leave the relationship, suddenly changes their position, even protecting their abuser. When this occurs, the power then shifts. The one who formerly had no power, suddenly becomes the powerful one who may now extract expressions of contrition, acts of restitution, and promises of change from the abuser -- often even resorting to violence.

Having extracted what she/he considers to be sufficient remorse and commitment to change, they then agree to, and often attempt, to protect the perpetrator from arrest and prosecution, believing that if they sufficiently nurture them, they will change, becoming the partner they always dreamed of.

This phenomenon occurs most often when legal or other intervention occurs some time after the episode of violence. The parties may be well into the honeymoon stage. In their shared feelings of mutuality, vulnerability and protectiveness, they may feel secure and really believe that "it will never happen again." Grasping onto that slim ray of hope -- that "love is sufficient to cover a multitude of sins" -- they deny reality and resist every form of assistance.

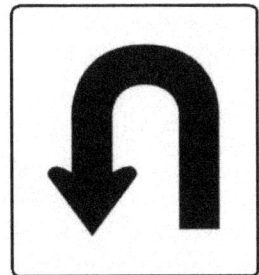

Changing abusive, violent behavior is perhaps best understood within the context and meaning of the word "repentance." To repent means much, much more than saying "I'm sorry." It goes beyond acknowledging one's mistakes. The word repentance literally means to turn around and go the other direction. It involves making a U-turn in life.

There are five well-defined steps in repentance: recognition, confession, accepting the consequences, restitution, and change:

- **Recognition** - Coming to a realization that our behavior, underlying values, attitudes and beliefs that allow such behavior are faulty, inconsistent with societal and moral norms, and need to be changed.

- **Confession** - Being open and honest, acknowledging our faults and misdeeds, admitting openly that "I did it," without justification or compromise.

- **Accepting the Consequences** - Accepting the punishment for the crime, and/or the acceptance of treatment as a substitute, or supplementation to, punishment. It involves more than a statement acknowledging one's error or even saying, "I was wrong and I deserve the punishment and/or treatment." It involves action, or restitution,

- **Restitution** - True restitution includes the ability to empathize with the abused and battered. It involves grieving, not because of one's punishment, but grieving for the pain of the sufferer, or victim. It even goes beyond grieving *for* the abused. It means to grieve *with* them -- to feel their pain and realize one's own contribution to that pain. Restitution includes a genuine desire to make the other whole, to make up to them for what they have suffered: to help restore them to wholeness. The level of restitution expressed, and how willingly it is proffered, is an excellent indicator of one's motivation to change and the prognosis of that change becoming reality.

- **Change** - Dropping denial, projection, isolation, justification and minimization; making a commitment to stop the violence and/or abuse immediately, regardless what the other person does or does not do; practicing with persistence new behavioral patterns; and pursuing with purpose new relationship dynamics. Well-established behavior patterns are never easy to change; however, it is virtually impossible if one does not develop a new goal or direction. As important as change is, it does not happen just by stopping what we have been doing.

Remember, *repentance* means "turning around and going the opposite direction." And, going the opposite direction means that we must have a different goal in mind, a different purpose, different objectives, and different behavioral patterns to achieve these new goals.

Goal Setting:
Goal setting can be one of the most difficult tasks imaginable if our life has been one of chaos and confusion. Persons who are caught up in a continuing saga of problems have usually lost sight of their life goals.

To paraphrase an old cliché' "when you're up to your waist in water fighting off the alligators, it's hard to remember that your original goal was to drain the swamp."

If you can imagine a person standing in a Florida swamp, flailing away at circling alligators, you can easily see that when our focus is on our problems, rather than our problems, our problems have quite literally become our goals. We become intent, as it were, seeking out and beating off the alligators, However, beating off the alligators, even if one were successful, will never be as effective as accomplishing the original goal of draining the swamp, which would eliminate the alligators' habitat.

What are *your* goals? Are they well established? Vague? Or nonexistent? Perhaps it would be well to remember the old adage, "If you aim for nothing, you are bound to hit it!"

Personal Application:
Describe your goals:

Personal:_____

Vocational:_____

Educational:_____

Relational:_____

Other:_____

The human mind functions somewhat like a computer. Computers operate on a principle called cybernetics. **Cybernetics** has to do with the concept of "teleology" referring to goal-striving, goal-oriented, preprogrammed or predetermined behavior. Cybernetics describes what is desired, what is necessary, and what happens in the process of a mechanical, electromechanical, or organic system achieving a predetermined goal.

Insofar as its function is concerned, man's central nervous system constitutes a marvelously complex cybernetic, goal-striving mechanism that functions very much like a built-in, automatic guidance system to achieve the goals one has predetermined or programmed themselves to achieve.

Personal Application:
How can understanding this help me reach my goals?

_____

_____

_____

Modern missiles and torpedoes are excellent examples of such guidance systems. They quite accurately describe the way that man himself achieves his goals. These guidance systems are called **servomechanisms**: mechanisms, or devices, that *automatically* serve mankind, making in-course corrections to reach a predetermined goal or target.

The trajectory of a missile or torpedo may, to the untrained eye, look like a direct, straight line, but in reality, the missile or torpedo is subject to drift due to air currents, ionosphere conditions, magnetic pull, heat waves, etc. It is brought back on course by numerous midcourse corrections effectuated by its guidance system. Moreover, the missile's target is rarely a static target. It too is moving -- often to avoid detection and/or damage.

Inside these guidance systems are various sensors (magnetic, heat, light, wind, sound, directional, etc.). Each sensor sends signals to the servomechanism advising that it is off course and that a certain midcourse correction is required. The servomechanism's direction is then altered to bring it back on course, capable of continuing its goal-seeking trajectory.

Compare this to an infant who reaches out to take hold of a toy. The infant's hand makes somewhat jerky motions, moving back and forth, until contact is made with the desired object or goal. As the child grows, his or her efforts become more accurate until at last, it looks like the child's hand reaches out in a straight line to grasps the desired object.

Personal Application:
If we have such a marvelous built-in system, why does mankind have such a hard time reaching their goals?

_____

_____

Years ago it was believed that an infant child lacked the necessary muscle coordination and that his or her "aim" was dependent on such muscle control. Sometimes later, it was thought that infants were born with limited vision and could not clearly discern their goal or the path traveled by their arm and hand. Both of these misbeliefs were, over time, proven inaccurate.

We now know that newborn children have perfect muscle coordination and perfect short-range vision. What they don't have is mature (adequately trained) "negative feedback." Negative feedback involves one's memory of attempts that did not achieve the desired result. This is the information required to make appropriate midcourse adjustments. As the child practices reaching for objects, his or her negative feedback database is constantly being expanded. In time, the child's midcourse corrections become finer and more frequent or greater in number. Eventually, it "looks" as though the child is reaching out in a straight line to grasp the desired article. This same concept guides mankind throughout life as he masters one task after another.

Personal Application:
What happens -- to man or machine -- if the object of their goals -- their predetermined destination is moved or externally altered?

Imagine for a moment the problems involved in achieving a goal if the goal is continually moved, worse yet, if one's goal is obscured.

Every cybernetic servomechanism -- man or machine -- will circle aimlessly if their goal (or target) is obscured. A homing pigeon, when released, flies in a circle several times to get its bearings, then takes off in a straight line toward home. A man lost in the woods also begins to circle [left-handed persons in a counterclockwise circle and right-handed persons in a clockwise circle], seemingly following a similar primitive instinct, but without the same highly developed homing system.

Mankind's "relational circling" is, however, very different. Having lost sight of his original goal, man tends to become "problem-focused," concentrating on his problem(s) rather than fixed on his goal(s). The unfortunate fact being, that the couple endlessly repeats the problematic behavior, since whatever occupies man's focus has, in reality, become his *goal.*

Focused on the very problem he or she wishes to eradicate, they repeat it over again and over again, circling through the same emotional "war-zone," experiencing the same negative results, time and time again!

Personal Application;
What personal and/or relational problems are you focused on that you would really like to be free from?

_____

_____

How can I break this cycle and pursue my chosen goals?

_____

_____

To break this destructive cycle, it is imperative that we get our focus off our problems and centered once again on our initial or reformed positive, fulfilling goal.

Personal Application;
What were your original personal, educational, vocational and relational goals when you entered your present partner relationship, vocational situation, etc.?

_____

_____

In all the years my wife and I have been counseling, we have never met a couple who entered into their relationship for the express purpose of having someone to fight and argue with. Unfortunately, however, many of find themselves continually engaged in that kind of activity. The primary reason being that two once loving, vision filled partners have lost sight of their original personal and relational goals and have begun focusing on their problems.

One of the quickest, most effective ways to reverse the destructive pattern of continuing conflict in a relationship is to refocus on original partnership goals. If you and your partner, you and your child, you and your employer/employee, etc., originally shared a common goal, begin to refocus on it. If you never had a goal beyond the immediate "conquest" and emotional high of a new lover or a new position, it is imperative that you now begin to establish one. Individuals in relationships of any kind, who do not share a a common goal (or vision) are rarely able to maintain their relationship for more than four or five years.

Many have lived the better part of their lives without meaningful, long-range goals. Others may have set short-range goals and then having achieved them, floundered around for a while then set other goals, often ones that take them in a different direction. Then, achieving those goals, they set still others, without having any real long-range goal, ultimate plan, purpose or direction.

Personal Application:
Why do I often fail to reach even my short- term goals?

_____

_____

Short-range goals most often fail due to the lack of long-range goals. Short-range goals are, in reality, more like the midcourse corrections effected by a guided missile to reach its long-range target. If we have no well defined long-range goal (or vision), our short-range goals are often inconsistent with one another and non-directional, causing us to circle, repeating the same old problems.

Personal Application:
If I've never had a vision of life -- and lack long-term (long-range) goals when and how do I begin to establish this?

Begin today to establish a long-range goal for your life. If you are in a spousal relationship, share your individual visions for life with one another. Then, working collaboratively, begin to develop a shared vision and long-range goals. If you have difficulty establishing long-range goals, imagine what you would like to be, what you would like to do, and perhaps where you would like to live, if time, talent, and resources were unlimited. Now, refine your goal to realistic limits and begin to focus on that goal.

Shortages of time, talent, resources, and other problems, are now converted to barriers between you and your goal that need to be removed or overcome. These apparent barriers then help define our constructive, short-range goals and guide is in taking the needed steps to remove these barriers, one by one.

Personal Application:
How can I use this information to improve my relationship?

Apply this concept of goal-setting to improving your spousal, parent-child and any other relationship. Develop or refine your shared vision. For example: Redefine your long-range goals for spousal harmony, intimacy, oneness and fulfillment with your partner. Covenant with each other to keep your focus on that goal, rather than on one another's performance. Identify the barriers between you and your goals, and implement positive plans remove each. Begin with your own negative behaviors, thoughts, speech, etc. You individually, and you and your partner as a couple, are marvelously complex, goal-striving servomechanisms. Once a vision is clarified, and a commitment to reach that goal made, your entire being (body, intellect, emotions, will and spirit) will begin working together *automatically* to reach the desired objective.

Personal Application:
What do I do about my partner and his or her need to change?

_____

_____

You can help your spouse achieve the same thing in their life (establish or clarify their vision and long-range goals), without them even realizing it. Take the initiative. Rather than focusing on, and commenting about his/her problems, gently and lovingly help them refocus on their own personal, and your common relational, vision and relationship goals. Affirm your partner, or other person, for each positive midcourse correction they make toward reaching their goals and realizing their vision for life.

Personal Application:
Setting New Goals: Remember the old adage, "If you aim for nothing, you are bound to hit it." Make a commitment that you will no longer act in an abusive, violent or conflictual and cantankerous manner toward your spouse, child, or other person. Repent, or turn away from your old, ineffective lifestyle. To accomplish this, it is imperative that you establish new goals -- goals your body, mind, and spirit can lock onto and strive toward. Consider how you would be treating your spouse, or other person, if your relationship was everything you originally envisioned it becoming. Now, understanding cause/effect relationships, begin treating the other person that way and watch your relationship improve.

List your long-range goals, making them as specific as possible; then identify the barriers that need removed for you to achieve each goal:

My personal goals are to:

_____

_____

The barriers that need removed are:

_____

_____

_____

My relationship goals are to:

_____

_____

_____

The barriers that need removed are:

_____

_____

_____

My vocational/educational goals are to:

_____

_____

The barriers that need removed are:

_____

_____

_____

Develop a plan for overcoming each of these barriers that is workable, and will enable you to reach your goals.

Homework Assignment -- Make a concentrated effort over the next week to list the positive characteristics, attributes, talents, and traits of your spouse or partner. Think of those things, perhaps, that attracted you to them in the very beginning of your relationship. Avoid focusing on the things that they do, or don't do, (their performance) that displease you. Focus instead on those traits and characteristics that make them a unique, one-of-a-kind, valuable person.

Traits and characteristics include: aspects of their physical appearance that please you; talents such as art, music, culinary skills, etc.; characteristics such as honesty, humor, integrity, dependability, reliability, trustworthiness, etc. Your partner, and all others you maintain relationships with, need to know that they are valued for who they are, rather than just for what they do.

Be especially careful not to put a "hook" on your statements (e.g., "I love your humor, _but_, or _except_ when it's about me," or "I love your hair, _but_ you don't keep it as nice as you used to.") Notice how the "hook" at the end of these statements virtually negates the effect of the original statement of appreciation and affirmation, actually inflicting new pain and injury.

Keep your affirmations short and positive.

_____

_____

_____

_____

_____

Homework Activity Exception:

Some persons may be taking this course as a result of a court order that includes a temporary restraining order. In this case, **DO NOT** violate a restraining order in an attempt to carry out this portion of this homework assignment. Instead, take time to write down your affirmative thoughts and date your letter(s). Take time on a regular basis to meditate of the positive characteristics listed and thank God that this person is in your life. If you and your partner are able to resolve your differences and restore your relationship, you may at that time share your letters and affirmations. They will still mean a great deal to them.

Personal Application

Take a few minutes to seek personal insight, asking God to search your heart to see if there is any iniquity therein that needs removed (Ps 139:23-24). If you are part of a recovery group, share your insight with the other members. Affirm those group members who were victims, as well as those who were the abusers but have demonstrated genuine remorse and have expressed a desire to restore a positive relationship. Strongly intervene when any member of your group tries to maintain innocence, justification, rationalization, minimization, etc., or who refuse to get their focus off of their partner's problems.

Don't allow members of your group, or yourself, to become involved in gender-bashing or stereotyping. These destroy the very concept of learning beyond one's behavior to see the other person as a unique, priceless soul. They also tend to reinforce one's negative focus on that person's perceived problem(s).

"Abstinence of Violence" Contract

Review the following abstinence of violence and abuse contract, and execute it as evidence of your commitment to change.

ABSTINENCE OF VIOLENCE CONTRACT

<u>I Understand this course will help me achieve the following:</u>

- To **STOP ACTS & THREATS OF VIOLENCE & ABUSE IMMEDIATELY.**

- To take personal responsibility for my own thoughts, feelings and behavior.

- To develop life-management skills in communication, conflict resolution, emotional and anger management.

- To practice and experience the effectiveness of "time-outs," emotional "temperature-taking," and positive internal dialogue (self-talk) corrections, and emotional coping skills.

- To develop healthful accountability to my group, my facilitator, and my significant other.

- To develop a new (nonviolent) self-concept and an improved self-worth.

<u>As a participant in this course, I agree that I will:</u>

- Stop threatening and/or committing all acts of violence and abuse against my spouse, all members of my family and others.

- Begin immediately to monitor my emotional temperature and take "time-out" when either my own or another's emotions begin to escalate.

- Participate fully in each lesson, completing all assignments and answering all personal application questions.

- Make-up any missed course work as a condition of my continued participation.

- Complete all class and homework assignments.

- Respect the confidence of other students and/or group members, discussing sensitive issues *only* with other group members and my instructor/facilitator. (i.e., What is shared here, stays here.)

- Accept personal responsibility for identifying those factors that have contributed to my past violent and abusive behavior.

- Be open to learn new skills to manage my fear, anger, frustration, fear, and conflict.

- Contact my instructor/facilitator, or other designated person, for assistance, *immediately* when any domestic conflict begins to escalate to a potentially dangerous level.

- Share any potentially dangerous conflicts that occur which required me to take a "time-out" with my mentor and/or group, openly discussing the situation, my thought processes, my reactions/responses, and the solution I employed in an effort to resolve the situation.

_____   _____

Client Signature   *Date*

Assignment: Make one or more copies of the next page. Place these time-out reminders in conspicuous places (i.e., next to your bathroom mirror, on the refrigerator door, etc.), and honor others by taking a time out whenever you sense your emotions beginning to escalate.

Don't Forget

Take A Time-out
when emotions
escalate

GLOSSARY

Continuum (p. 15) - A line between two opposing positions or states of being.

Acculturalization (p. 15) - Habituated to, or respond to, stimuli in a certain manner.

Intrinsic (p. 15) - Inherent, inborn or ingrained.

Divergent (p. 15) - Different, dissimilar, unlike each other.

Implicit (p. 15 - Unexpressed but understood

Explicit (p. 15) - Expressed, clear-cut and unambiguous.

Dissipated (p. 15) - Faded, weakened or dissolved.

Reinforcement (p. 16) - To strengthen

Feign (p. 16) - Pretend, counterfeit, fake.

Perpetrator (p. 16) - Offender, violator, criminal

Intervention (p. 16) - Interference, interruption

Phenomenon (p. 16) - Wonderment, event not clearly understood.

Vulnerability (p. 16) - Susceptible to exposure

Repentance (p. 17) - Remorse motivating change.

Cybernetics (p. 18) - Goal oriented, or goal-striving.

Servomechanism (p. 18) - Devices designed to make in-course corrections in direction or function.

Affirm (p. 20 -- Approve, confirm, strengthen by declaration.

Gender-bashing (p. 20) - Stereotyping either gender (male or female) in a negative, derogatory manner.

Stereotyping (p. 20) - Judging all similar people, places and/or things according to one's familiarity with a single or small sample.

Unique (p. 20) - Incomparable, matchless, one of a kind.

KEY POINTS

- **The three phases in the cycle of violence:**
    - Tension-building
    - Release, or explosive
    - Honeymoon, or remorse

- **Phase One Triggers**

- **Gender differences in communication**

- **Differences in length of phases between types of violence**

- **Differences in Honeymoon phase between types of violence**

- **"He who has the most to lose has the greatest power"**
  How does this old proverb apply to domestic violence?

- **Name the five steps of repentance**

- **Goal setting**

- **Memorize and understand this proverb:**

  "If you aim for nothing, you're bound to hit it."

CHAPTER FOUR
UNDERSTANDING ABUSE

Power and Control Survey

(Identify the various form/s of power and control abuse used by each family member as you review the text, and place a check under the person who used, or uses this destructive technique)

Method	Self	Partner	Father	Mother
Spiritual Abuse				
Sexual Abuse				
Verbal Abuse				
Emotional Abuse				
Intellectual Abuse				
Intimidation				
Threats				
Silence				
Environmental Abuse				
Isolation				
Gender Privilege				
Triangulation				
Financial Abuse				
Responsibility Abuse				
Substance Abuse				
Stalking				
Property Destruction				
Physical Abuse				
# of methods used =>				

Personal Application:
Describe, in your own words, your understanding of domestic and/or family abuse:

_____

_____

Definition of Abuse

The principle meaning of the word abuse is "misuse" -- referring to the misapplication, or erroneous use, of something that, if properly applied, would reap positive results. In abusive relationships, this applies to the misuse of love -- love being the very essence of spousal, parent/child and most other relationships.

When distorted, the "power of love" becomes the "love of power." Those who exercise this substitution for "love" usually believe that power and control are essential to relationship success. They believe, for example, that the husband *must* be the "king of the castle," the wife *ought* to be in submission -- even subservient, children are to be seen and not heard, etc.

Personal Application:
What is the driving force in abusive relationships that contributes to power and control issues and resulting incidents of violence?

_____

POWER AND CONTROL WHEEL

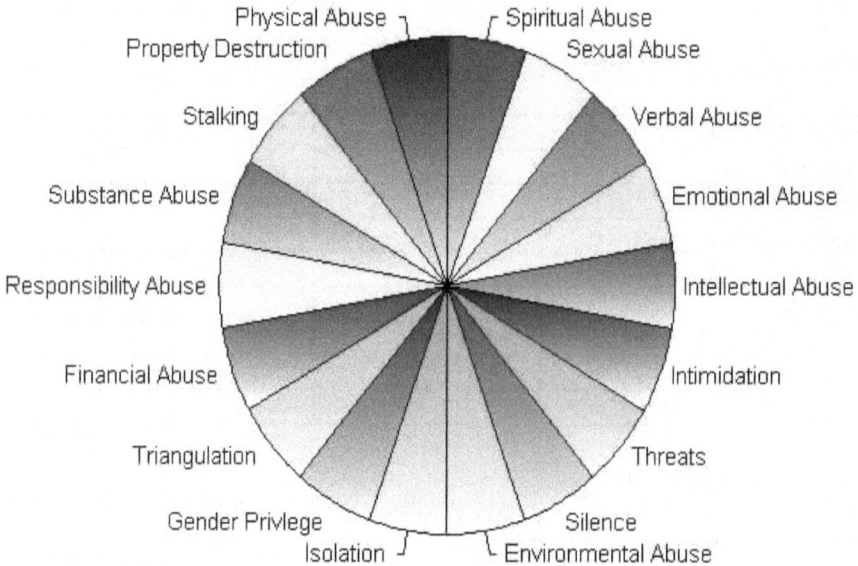

Physical Abuse
Property Destruction
Spiritual Abuse
Sexual Abuse
Stalking
Verbal Abuse
Substance Abuse
Emotional Abuse
Responsibility Abuse
Intellectual Abuse
Financial Abuse
Intimidation
Triangulation
Threats
Gender Privlege
Silence
Isolation
Environmental Abuse

At a subconscious level, one or both parties in abusive relationships, usually believe that "if no one is *in control* then everything will be *out of control*." This, in their perception would be disastrous. With little or no understanding of the power of love, many husbands and wives, lovers, parents and friends seek to maintain their relationships and prevent problems through sheer power and control. Power and control issues may be manifest in one or more ways. The more prevalently used methods are depicted on the *Power and Control Wheel* illustrated above.

Take time to examine this power and control wheel, identifying the forms of abuse that you or others in your family of origin and present family use, or have used. After identifying these, check those you used and those you believe others used, in the table at the beginning of this chapter. After doing so. read the following descriptions of each form of abuse. Now, after reading the descriptions of each form of abuse. Take time to reconsider which forms of abuse you use, or have used, and which types have been used against you. Compare your revelation with your initial perception identified in the survey, on the first page of this chapter. As you complete this, you will see that when families begin to use power and control to govern their relationships, everyone in the family gets caught up in this maladaptive relationship dynamic.

RELATIONSHIP ABUSES DEFINED

Spiritual Abuse - Spiritual abuse is anything that abuses a person deep enough to wound or close their spirit -- that deep inner core, or center of one's being. Spiritual wholeness is largely about that deep inner sense of being loved and lovable. Conversely, spiritual distress, or disease, reflects one's sense of being rejected and unloved.

Personal Application:
At what age, and through what action or inaction, does spiritual abuse most often begin?

_____

_____

Spiritual abuse can, and most often does, begin in the womb. If a child is unwanted, the unborn child will sense this as severe rejection and the absence of love. This results in this child coming into the world spiritually wounded. The sense of being unwanted doesn't happen only in cases where the mother absolutely didn't want to become pregnant or carry the baby to term. It can occur also under circumstances such as war, famine, or when the mother has been abandoned by the father. Such circumstances experienced give mothers cause for grave concern about childbearing. Research indicates that this concern is felt by the unborn infant, wounding his/her spirit. Intrauterine wounding of the spirit is most often manifest as a sense of rejection, worthlessness, a lack of significance, or very low self-esteem.

Personal Application:
When is a person most susceptible to spiritual abuse?

_____

Spiritual wounds can be inflicted at any time throughout life. Children during the first eighteen months of life are particularly susceptible. Young children are wholly dependent during this stage and must look to their primary caregivers, usually their mother and father, to provide all their basic needs. A child's primary developmental task during early childhood involves learning trust, hope, faith and love. If their needs are not met, children learn to mistrust, rather than trust; they develop hopelessness rather than hopeful expectations; they are impaired in their ability to exercise faith and tend to substitute lust for love. Children who perceive a lack in their needs being met, their desires being unfulfilled, as rejection and a lack of love.

As one grows older, the spirit can be wounded in other ways. Preschool and school age children may experience spiritual abuse with a different twist. They may experience rejection as a result of others' looks and gestures of acceptance or lack thereof. For example, a child who is the only one of their ethnicity, or religion, in their neighborhood, church or school, may be rejected by other children. Others are rejected due to learning and/or developmental difficulties, questions about their parentage, national origin or cultural diversity.

Later in life, people often experience rejection from others because their spiritual beliefs, their perceptions and opinions differ from their parents,' their peers' or life-partners'. Insensitive parents and/or partners often unconsciously inflict spiritual abuse through their outright rejection of the other' persons spiritual beliefs, values, salvation experience and individual spiritual growth.

Personal Application;
In what other way do adults frequently abuse their partners spiritually, by employing religious beliefs and values?

_____

_____

Spouses often inflict spiritual abuse on another by openly rejecting and demeaning the other's spirituality. It is not uncommon for partners to verbally beat up on one another, citing quotations from the Bible or other sacred texts in an attempt to prove themselves superior to the other. Denying the validity of another person's spiritual experience and/or spirituality, because it is different from one's own, is one of the most severe forms of spiritual abuse. This effectively results in a rejection of the person for who they are at the very core of their being.

Personal Application:
Describe any spiritual abuse you have experienced and/or inflicted against another person:

_____

_____

_____

Sexual Abuse   - The abuse, or "misuse" of another's sexuality. Sexual abuse, is nearly as devastating as spiritual abuse since mankind's core identity is comprised of his/her spirituality and sexuality, which are inextricably intertwined.

Personal Application:
What are some of the more common effects of sexual abuse?

_____

_____

Sexual abuse fractures a person's core-identity, severely damaging their self-worth. Those who have experienced sexual abuse generally feel inferior or somehow "less-than" their peers. They often experience a sense of worthlessness, purposelessness and powerlessness in life. They frequently feel damaged and suffer profound shame, believing that if others *really* knew what had happened to them, they could not possibly love or accept them.

Sexual abuse also contributes to numerous personality disorders. Research indicates that sexual abuse is one of the leading contributors to disorders such as Borderline Personality Disorder,

Posttraumatic Stress Disorder, Schizoaffective Disorders, Clinical Depression, Avoidant Personality Disorder, Agoraphobia and Social Phobia, Substance Abuse, and a host of other disorders.

Personal Application:
Sexual abuse is usually thought of in the terms of incest and molestation. What is the difference? Which is the most damaging? Why?

_____

_____

Sexual abuse, against a child, commonly involves incest and/or molestation. Incest is defined as the improper expression of sex between family members. It is the more devastating of the two, since it involves the violation of a sacred trust as well as the violation of one's personal boundaries, their physical, spiritual and soulish well-being. Molestation is defined as improper sexual expression by a non-family member. It is also very damaging, but normally does not involve the same level of trust violation as incest.

Personal Application:
What acts, other than penetration, constitute sexual abuse and, what determines which form of abuse is most damaging to one's personhood?

_____

_____

Sexual abuse of a child does not have to involve digital or penile penetration, fellatio or cunnilingus (oral stimulation of the genitals) to cause severe damage. Fondling a child's genitals, and even some misguided parents' practice of requiring a child to pull down his/her pants to be spanked, thus exposing them, often results in severe emotional damage in children.

The attachment bond between a child and his/her abuser (i.e., the closeness of their relationship), as well as the duration, frequency and forcefulness involved in any form of sexual abuse, collectively determine the severity of resulting personhood damage.

Personal Application:
What are some of the adult effects of childhood sexual abuse?

_____

_____

Children who have been sexualized at an early age, and/or abused over an extended period of time, become habituated to the abuse and grow up lacking healthy sexual boundaries. As adolescents they often live very promiscuous lives. As adults, these individuals often find themselves in sexually abusive relationships involving their abuse of others and/or their being re-abused themselves. Women who were sexually abused as children often experience much more severe premenstrual stress (PMS) than other women. Each month these women are subconsciously reminded of their femininity, their vulnerability and their early-life abuse.

Men and women who were themselves abused as children are much more likely to act out in a sexually improper manner with children than are those who were not thus abused. [Research among prison populations in the US indicates that more than 95% of those convicted of pedophillia (the sexual abuse of children) were themselves similarly abused as children. Moreover, pedophiles most frequently act out against children who are approximately the same age they were when abused.]

Men and women who were sexually abused as children tend to have a great deal of other-sex ambivalence (women against men and men against women). Ambivalence is the fusion of the opposing emotions. The effect of this is that when one emotion is felt the other sense is aroused as well. Childhood sexual abuse often results in the fusion of love and hate, fear and sexual arousal, rage and sexual arousal. The fusion of love and hate severely damages healthy conjugal relationships, leading to love-hate relationships. The fusion of fear and sexual arousal damages one's ability to reach normal orgasm since when aroused the person concurrently feels fear, which leads to impotence. Similarly, the fusion of anger or rage and sexual arousal, that is common when force is used during sexual abuse, commonly leads to sex offender behavior such as voyeurism, exhibitionism and rape.

Personal Application:
Who is responsible for the majority of childhood sexual abuse?

_____

_____

_____

Until quite recently, it was believed that the typical profile of a child sexual predator, or pedophile, was male, most often a relative, (usually fathers, stepfathers, and brothers) or a close family friend. Current research seems to contradict some of these perceptions. This research indicates that while most sexual abusers know the child they abuse, they are not relatives. In fact, about 60% of perpetrators are non-relative acquaintances, such as a single mother's boyfriends, a friend of the family, a baby-sitter, or neighbor. Only about 30% of those who sexually abuse children are relatives of the child, such as fathers, uncles, or cousins. Strangers are perpetrators in about 10% of child sexual abuse cases.

Sexual abuse by women of children and teens is a subject that most parents and caregivers are not familiar with. Female sexual predators frequently go unreported because of a lack of awareness by the public. Research indicates that 55% to 75% of sexual predators are male and 25% to 45% are female. The reporting problem stems from the fact that 86% of the victims identifying a female as their sexual predators aren't believed, so their crimes go unreported and they are not prosecuted.

As recently as 10 years ago, it was a common assumption that females did not, or could not, sexually abuse children or youth. Many professionals working in the field believed that women represented only about 1% to 3% of sexual abusers at most. Mounting evidence about sexual abuse perpetration at the hands of teen and adult females has begun to challenge our assumptions, though these earlier outdated views still tend to predominate.

The percentage of women and teenage girl perpetrators recorded in case report studies is small and ranges from 3% to 10% (Kendall-Tackett and Simon, 1987; McCarty, 1986; Schultz and Jones, 1983; Wasserman and Kappel, 1985). When the victim is male, female perpetrators account for 1 % to 24% of abusers. When the victim is female, female perpetrators account for 6% to 17% of abusers (American Humane Association, 1981; Finkelhor and Russell, 1984; Finkelhor et al., 1990).

In six studies reviewed by Russell and Finkelhor, female perpetrators accounted for 25% or more of abusers. Ramsay-Klawsnik (1990) found that adult females were abusers of males 37% of the time and female adolescents 19% of the time. Both of these rates are higher than the same study reported for adult and teen male abusers. There is some evidence that females are more likely to be involved with co-abusers, typically a male, although studies report a range from 25% to 77% (Faller, 1987; Kaufman et al., 1995; McCarty, 1986).

Self-report studies provide a very different view of sexual abuse than that which society has held. In a retrospective study of male victims, 60% reported being abused by females (Johnson and Shrier, 1987). The same rate was found in a sample of college students (Fritz et al., I 981). In other studies of male university and college students, rates of female perpetrators were found at levels as high as 72% to 82% (Fromuth and Burkhart, 1987, 1989; Seidner and Calhoun, 1984).

Bell et al. (1981) found that 27% of males were abused by females. In some of these types of studies, females represent as much as 50% of sexual abusers (Risin and Koss, 1987). Knopp and Lackey (1987) found that 51% of victims of female sexual abusers were male. It is evident that case report and self-report studies yield very different types of data about prevalence. These extraordinary differences tell us we need to start questioning all of our assumptions about perpetrators and victims of child maltreatment.

Finally, there is an alarmingly high rate of sexual abuse by females in the backgrounds of rapists, sex offenders and sexually aggressive men - 59% (Petrovich and Templer, 1984), 66% (Groth, 1979) and 80% (Briere and Smiljanich, 1993).

Personal Application:
What types of behavior constitutes sexual abuse in adult relationships?

_____

_____

Sexual abuse in a spousal relationship is, unfortunately, very common. It is one of the more devastating forms of abusive power and control. The abuse may be in the form of forcing one's partner to participate in sex, demanding that they perform demeaning or undesirable forms of sexual fulfillment or, it may manifest itself in the other extreme -- the intentional withholding of sexual pleasure and fulfillment, in an effort to punish and/or control one's partner.

Then again, the abuse may take place in the form of sexual harassment. One or the other may make course, vulgar jokes about the other's gender and sexuality or about their sexual performance. The abuser may also make uninvited and unwelcome sexual advances at times and in places that are deemed unacceptable.

Personal Application:
What is the effect of engaging in sex to make up after a fight?

_____

_____

A man -- or woman -- who insists that their partner have sex after a fight; whether as an extension of the violence or in an attempt to "make-up," is guilty of sexual abuse. The abused partner: most often the wife, may submit -- not out of love but out of fear -- in an effort to avoid further abuse. The abused person needs comfort, nurture and care, but what they need most is emotional nurture, comfort and time to heal. They need this much more than they need, or desire, sexual fulfillment. If their partner forces sex on them, and they gives in, they will as a result, experience an increased sense of helplessness, powerlessness and personhood degradation.

Personal Application:
Identify the things that men often do or say that may seems sexually abusive to a woman?

_____

_____

Many men have been "socialized" to perceive of women as mere sex objects to be conquered for _their_ personal enjoyment and fulfillment. This perception encourages men to view women as instruments, or tools, designed for his sexual satiation. These men often incorporate sexual violence into their behavior as an effort to maintain masculine dominance, power and control.

A man is also sexually abusing his wife when he expects her to provide him with sexual fulfillment after she has observed him flirting with another woman; after he accuses her of "sleeping around," or "coming-on" to another man; and, after he calls her degrading, depersonalizing or dehumanizing names such as "slut," "cunt," "bitch," "whore," "pig." etc. These things are designed to manipulate her into becoming involved in sexual activities against her will, but lead to resentment, bitterness and hatred.

Conversely, in what ways do women often, perhaps unconsciously, sexually abuse men?

_____

A commonly held view of heterosexuality is that men are always wanting and seeking sex with females; that males are designed to

58

be dominant, while females are supposed to be submissive. It is generally purported that men initiate sexual encounters, and women accept or decline male invitations for sex. It is also commonly believed that if a female initiates sexual contact with a male, this is viewed as a rare and exciting opportunity that no man should let pass by; in fact he should gratefully participate.

Given these misbeliefs, many people see nothing wrong with a woman pursuing a boy or man sexually. In fact, in some circles it is considered a good way to introduce boys to heterosexuality. Some fathers, relying on this misbelief, take their young sons to prostitutes with the mistaken belief that it is "good" for them. Movies, stories, jokes, and fantasies portraying older women sexually "seducing" young boys abound, most presenting it in positive terms.

What effect does this have on men who were sexually abused by women?

Sadly, many men who were sexually abused by women live their lives locked in silence, shame, and self-loathing. Society tells them that not only was their experience not abusive, they should have enjoyed it, and if they didn't, there must be something terribly wrong with them. Even when these experiences are recognized as abuse, these men may be viewed as having been "weak" or "not man enough" because they were unable, or unwilling, to stop it, defend themselves, or put it behind them.

The myth that men can't be victimized sexually, particularly by women, is firmly entrenched in many cultures. Many men who dare acknowledge that they were sexually abused by women are often cruelly laughed at and humiliated. Most men dare say a word about such abuse for fear of feeling even more ashamed than they already feel.

Many men who were sexually abused by women feel deeply ashamed of themselves, their sexuality, and their gender. Sadly and mistakenly, they believe that there must be something profoundly wrong with them that resulted in them being abused in this way. Some men defend against these feelings by being in a constant state of anger or rage - one of the few emotions that is socially acceptable for men. Many male survivors cope with the abuse by drinking, using drugs, living recklessly, avoiding intimate relationships, numbing out their feelings by dissociating or using alcohol or drugs. Often, they experience depression, anxiety, panic attacks and episodes of poorly controlled anger. Others live a reactive lifestyle, taking out their anger on other females in the form of rape, sexual harassment or other forms of abuse.

Last, but not least, another form of sexual abuse that is common in spousal relationships occurs when one repeatedly awakens their partner from sound sleep to demand sex.

Personal Application:
What is one of the more common passive-aggressive methods employed in sexual abuse?

_____

Women and men who intentionally withhold sexual fulfillment from their spouse in a manipulative fashion to get their own way or in an attempt to punish their spouse for other, non-related, issues are also practicing sexual abuse.

Verbal Abuse - Verbal abuse is any attempt to control, or gain power over, another person through one's verbal communication. It usually results in emotional and spiritual abuse but has pronounced aspects not seen in other forms of abuse, sufficient to warrant separate consideration. Relationship fulfillment is based on mutuality, which is the polar opposite of dominance. Regardless of how one seeks to exercise dominance over another person, it is abuse.

Personal Application:
What aspects of maltreatment are common in verbal abuse?

_____

In verbal abuse the dominance occurs not so much in _what_ is said, but rather in _how_ it is said. Verbal abusers are master manipulators. They use the inflection (tone, volume, pitch, pressure and clarity -- or lack thereof) in their voice to control and dominate others. Verbal abusers also use an abundance of subtle psychological defenses that keep their victim confused, powerless and discouraged.

60

They use defense mechanisms such as projection (attributing their own thoughts, feelings and actions to the other); minimization and/or maximization (making things seem much more significant or insignificant than they really are); unintelligible speech (intentional mumbling, slurred speech and/or talking below the level of the other person's hearing); and unexpected, frightening outbursts.

Verbal abusers often seek to wear the other person down by filibustering (maintaining a verbal barrage that overwhelms the other person), or by having "their say," then disconnecting with comments such as "end of discussion." Verbal abusers are masters in the use of dirty fighting techniques, such as taking advantage of the other in the timing of an argument, criticism, name calling, making humiliating remarks, mocking, redirecting, interrupting, etc. [We will discuss these dirty fighting techniques in greater detail in a later lesson.]

Personal Application:
What is a good way to tell whether you or your partner are being verbally abusive?

_____

_____

Good criteria one can use to determine whether or not verbal abuse is a problem in your relationships include the following:

* Would someone listening in think that our conversation sounded like two friends visiting?

* Is it easy for you to imagine yourself talking like the other person?

* Is it easy for you to imagine the other person talking to you like you talk to them?

* Does your conversation demonstrate a mutual good will and genuine effort to understand each other's view point?

* Is your conversation aimed at understanding, and free from blaming, shaming and/or faultfinding?

* Does either party feel as though he or she is on the witness stand being interrogated?

- Does either frequently interrupt or correct the other, attempting to reframe their information, alter their perception, or redefine their reality?

- Does either party use insincere, dry, or cutting humor against the other?

- Does either party disparage, put down, or demean the other person's talents, traits, capabilities, looks, experience, etc.?

- Does either of you invade your partner's quiet time and/or private space?

Personal Application:
Does your partner ever tell you that you are abusing them verbally, yet you think you're acting okay?

_____

Many verbal abusers believe they are the "good guy" because they never "act" inappropriately. They cannot understand why their partner gets so angry -- angry enough to become abusive in ways that are more easily recognized as expressions of abuse such as physical abuse or the destruction of property.

Personal Application;
Have you ever felt abused but wondered if you really were or just imagined it?

_____

Persons who are verbally abused are often confused and depressed. They may feel helpless, hopeless, and purposeless, yet not really knowing whether or not they are abused. Their very reality has been so distorted, so convoluted, by the other's constant verbal harangue, they are bewildered. This confusion, together with the abuser's high use of projection, results in the near destruction of their personhood.

One of the surest ways to destroy another's perception, to unravel that connective thread between one's inner and outer realities, between action and result, cause and effect, thought and expression, is to abuse a person verbally, while at the same time attempting to make that person feel responsible for the abuse he or she is receiving (Evans, 1993). Common attempts to achieve this include statements such as: "you make me behave this way."

62

Emotional Abuse - Emotional abuse is perhaps the most common form of abuse in both spousal and parent/child relationships.

Emotional abuse is defined as any activity that attacks the self-worth and/or the self-identity or self-image of another.

Personal Application:
What is the most common underlying reason for attacking another verbally?

_____

Emotional abusers usually have vague, poorly formed or fractured self-identities and a correspondingly low self-worth. They seek to overcompensate for these weaknesses by holding power and dominance over their partner, children and others. They lack the inner security and skills necessary to develop and maintain intimate relationships, and tend to "relate" to others as objects rather than their equals. Most emotional abusers have themselves experienced substantial emotional abuse. As a result of the abuse experienced, they have developed deep ambivalence, simultaneously feeling a compulsion to change and punish those they attempt to relate to, when their response fails to meet their expectations.

Personal Application:
What personality distortion tends to drive a person to exercise control over those they love?

_____

This distortion is the duality often referred to as the "Dr. Jekyll and Mr. Hyde" personality. It results from the abuser seeking to gain control over their own felt powerlessness through their overt control of their partner, children, the environment, etc.

Emotional abusers are master controllers, able to turn their manipulating behavior on and off at will in order to punish and control their partner, while simultaneously looking like a loving, caring husband or wife to the outside world. Emotional abusers are capable of interrupting a seemingly "uncontrollable" episode of rage with their spouse, answer the phone or a knock on the door, and carry on a happy conversation with an outsider. Then, when the outsider leaves or the phone call ends, they resume the episode of rage directed against their partner as though there had never been a break.

Personal Application:
Have you ever been told that you have a Dr. Jekyll -- Mr. Hyde type personality? Or, are you, or have you been, in a relationship with one who manifested this Dr. Jekyll -- Mr. Hyde duality? _____

If so, identify the person(s) exhibiting this duality: _____

_____

The abuser's own felt helplessness to change is commonly projected on the abused as his/her "chosen" scapegoat! Emotional put-downs, demeaning others, withholding emotional affirmation, ridicule and insult, mind-games, and mental coercion are the emotional abuser's chief relationship "skills." [These, and similar approaches, termed "dirty-fighting-techniques," are discussed in great detail in a later lesson.]

Personal Application:
What is the emotional abuser's real purpose in putting others down?

_____

_____

The emotional abuser may employ any number of approaches or techniques to accomplish his/her ends. However, his/her *true* purpose in demeaning others is to elevate themselves by making the other person feel powerless and "less than." Emotional abuse may emanate out of a conflict; however, its true purpose is never about conflict resolution. Emotional abuse is, in reality, about the abuser's refusal to address and resolve conflict. It is the use of raw power and control to get one's own way, while ignoring the needs and desires of the other person.

Personal Application:
Describe the damage done to your relationships through your own or another's emotional abuse?

_____

_____

_____

Intellectual Abuse - Intellectual abuse is unquestionably a form of emotional abuse, yet it has characteristics that are distinct enough to require separate

64

consideration. Intellectual abuse involves the use of power and control in an attempt to dominate the other person intellectually, launching out to establish one's own mental superiority by demeaning the other person's intelligence, general knowledge, vocabulary, method, or speed of information processing, etc.

Personal Application:
How does intellectual abuse differ from emotional abuse?

_____

_____

Intellectual abusers draw biting comparisons between their own and the other person's level of education, the institutions of higher learning attended, their knowledge of specific subjects, memories of specific incidents, etc. Their express intent is to make the other person feel incompetent and/or at least confused, thereby disqualifying their opinions, beliefs, decisions, judgments, etc. The abuser's primary goal is to instill a sense of helplessness and dependence in the abused person, sufficient in intensity to subordinate them, destroy their personal integrity, and secure their intellectual bondage.

Personal Application:
In what way have you used intellectual abuse? And, against whom?

_____

Intimidation: Personal Application:

Describe your understanding of intimidation:

_____

Intimidation is a form of abuse that employs both verbal and nonverbal aspects of communication, used to inflict fear, confusion and self-doubt in the other person. The intimidation abuser's communication "skills" usually incorporate an abundance of cursing; vulgarity; loud, coarse, biting speech; continual circular and often nonsensical reasoning; relentless arguing; menacing looks, gestures and actions.

Personal Application:
What is the intimidator's real intent?

_____

The abuser's intent is to manipulate, to get his/her own way at any cost. Their 'game' is designed to inflict feelings of guilt and shame, and a sense of obligation in the abused.

Personal Application:
Identify the techniques the intimidator employs in an attempt to carry out his/her intent?

_____

The intimidation abuser persists in getting in the last word, insisting that he/she is always right. They make up impossible rules and regulations, and impose these rules and unrealistic expectations on others. They frequently change the rules and their expectations in an effort to maintain their superiority and the others' sense of confusion.

Personal Application:
In what ways have you intimidated others?

_____

_____

Threat Abuse:

Personal Application:
How do threats differ from intimidation?

_____

The abuser that employs this form of maltreatment will use virtually any form of personhood revilement that he or she can think up. Threatening to end the relationship is perhaps the most common; however, threats to inflict physical injury, to take the children, to destroy personal property, to report real, imagined or concocted events to family members, employers and authorities are also common.

Personal Application:
What does this person's often use as his/her ultimate threat?

_____

_____

If other threats are unsuccessful in getting his/her own way, the threat abuser frequently threatens self-harm or suicide, blaming the abused for driving him or her to the point of self-destruction and making sure they understand that they will be eternally responsible for their demise.

Silence Abuse - The abuser that employs silence, often called the **"Silent Knight,"** intentionally uses silence as a weapon -- referred to as the "violence of silence."

Personal Application;
What is the most common reason for an individual giving another person the 'silent treatment?"

_____

_____

The Silent Knight usually lacks communication and conflict-resolution skills and the ability to adequately express his or her emotions. In defense of his/her own personhood, the Silent Knight reacts to frustration by intentionally closing his/her spirit to the other person, refusing to communicate. They may even fail to acknowledge the other's attempts to engage them in communication and conflict resolution.

The Silent Knight becomes a master at ignoring his or her significant other. He/she employs the skill of snubbing, shunning, rebuffing, and spurning the other as a means to avoid conflict resolution; to further punish, control, demean, debase, degrade, and annihilate their partner's self-worth and fracture their self-identity. They may keep at it for days in order to gain their own way or punish the other person for some real or imagined injustice.

Personal Application:
What are the more common outcomes of this form of abuse?

_____

Whatever the reason for his/her imposed silence, the result of the Silent Knight's behavior is the destruction of their spouse's serenity, identity and reality. Ultimately, it may contribute to the destruction of the relationship itself.

Environmental Abuse - Personal Application:
How would you describe an environmental abuser?

_____

Environmental abusers take advantage every opportunity to control the abused person's environment. They demand and exercise control over the temperature in the home or automobile, the television programs their partner and children watch, where they go when dining out, what music they listen to, the entertainment they engage in, etc.

They dictate the placement of furniture in the home, the type and placement of items of decor, plantings in the yard, the type of vehicles the family has, etc. They often lay ownership claim to items that in reality belong to the whole family. For example: there is often "dad's chair" that no one else dare sit in; dad controls the TV remote when he's home; mom claims the kitchen is hers and becomes angry if dad even thinks of invading _her_ domain.

Personal Application:
What forms of environmental abuse exist in your home and family?

_____

_____

The environmental abuser's actions may be either overt (clearly evident and aggressively controlling), or covert (underhanded, such as refusing to participate with his/her partner or family members unless everything is done their way). Environmental abusers seem to live by the motto, "it's my way or the highway."

Personal Application:
How often have you used this or a similar cliché' in an attempt to get your own way?

Isolation Abuse - Isolation may take one of two forms: isolation of self or isolation of one's partner or other person. Either form is an effort to impose manipulative power and control. If the abuser employs self-isolation, he/she may lock themselves in the bedroom or bathroom, either refusing to communicate at all, or repeatedly taunting the person on the other side of the barricade. Self-isolation may escalate to grand proportions, with the abuser leaving the home for days to punish and gain control. In a similar fashion to locking out the other person, the abuser may leave and maintain complete silence, or may call from time to time to taunt and torment the abused.

Personal Application:
Describe self-isolation patterns practiced in your home:

When the abuser elects to isolate his/her partner, a completely different pattern is implemented. The abuser employs every technique at his/her disposal to isolate, cutoff, infuriate, intimidate and inflict fear in the other by limiting their access to other people. The abuse may be as "mild" as "demanding" that the other be constantly in their presence, controlling what the other person does or says, whom he or she sees or talks to, listening in on or limiting phone calls, and controlling where he/she goes through continual introjection and intimidation.

Or, it may include more severe acts such as threatening the other's family and friends, disabling or destroying the person's phone or sabotaging their vehicle In extreme cases, isolation of one's partner may include tying the person up, or locking them in a closet or room. In bizarre cases we have encountered in our counseling experience, abuse victims have been locked in barns, sheds, and attics. In one case that we were called to intervene in, a woman was locked in an outside, oversize bird cage for several days, by her "boyfriend," to effect her isolation, cutoff her support and keep her from seeking refuge.

Personal Application:
Describe any incidents in your family where someone has been isolated by another person:

_____

Triangulation Abuse - Triangulation is the technical term for one of the more subtle but destructive forms of abuse in spousal and other intimate relationships. Triangulation is, in reality, the disruption of the normal "triangle" between parents and their children where one person -- usually one of the parents -- is cut off from the other parent and children, resulting in an unnatural bonding developing between the children and one parent.

For example, an abusive husband may make his wife feel guilty about her care and concern for the children. He may tell the children that their mother is crazy, and may use them as messengers to convey demeaning or demanding messages back and forth, thus continuing the battle without "personal" involvement. He may also use child support as a leverage to get his way, or "punish" her for leaving him or denying him sex.

Conversely, the wife may say to her husband, "_we_ hate you," implicating the children in her personal feelings in an effort to hurt and punish her husband. She may also use the children to convey hurtful messages to her husband, or in the heat of a conflict may even grab the children and say "come on kids, '_we_' are leaving." The abusive aspect of these actions is that she is not doing this to protect the children, but to carry on her power and control struggle with her husband.

Personal Application:
Describe any triangulation patterns that exist in your present family, or that existed in your family of origin:

_____

Personal Application:
What effect does triangulation have on the children?

_____

In families employing triangulation, the children are caught up in the destructive game and used as tools. Children used in this manner are themselves being abused. Even worse, these children are being taught some of the most destructive forms of family violence, including manipulation and child abuse. Some research indicates that triangulation contributes to sexual identity confusion and homosexuality.

Gender Privilege - Gender privilege is a form of abuse that both men and women employ in their attempt to exercise power and control over the other person, family events, circumstances, etc. The husband may treat his wife as a servant, expecting her to meet his every need and desire. He may assert his misbelief that it is "the husband's right and/or responsibility to make all the important decisions" or remind her that he is "the master of the castle" and that it is the "duty" of the wife to submit. He may spend substantial time with his men friends while denying her similar privileges with her friends.

He may refuse any accountability to his wife while in return demanding that she be accountable to him in everything. He maintains a dual standard concerning husbands' and wives' rights.

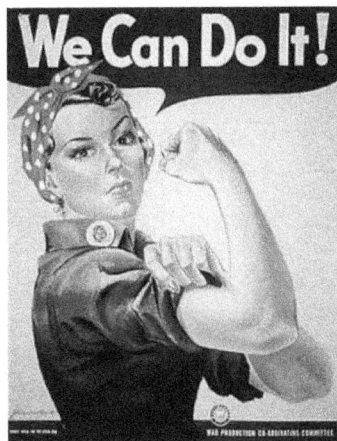

Wives, on the other hand, also employ gender abuse issues to control. She may attempt to show her husband that she doesn't need him by attempting to do his work first or better, then rub it in. Or, she may feign an inability to do certain things because, after all, "I am only a woman." She may demand that he make the decisions she feels uncomfortable with, or press him to punish the children for the misbehavior *she* observed. She may even develop a pattern of hypocrondrasis (always pretending to be sick), demanding that he do everything for her because she is too "ill."

Personal Application:
Describe any patterns of gender abuse that exist in your family, or that existed in your family of origin?

_____

_____

Financial Abuse - The financial abuser controls his/her partner by maintaining control over all of the family's resources. He/she may demand that the other stay home with them (if the family income is sufficient, or if the abused receives Social Security or similar benefits), the abuser may demand that the other person stay home with the children while they work outside the home.

The financial abuser may do everything possible to keep his/her partner from getting or keeping a job. They may, instead of this, refuse to work to support the family. The financial abuser often insists that they are the "responsible one," demanding that the other person turn over all of their income or other assets for them to manage. The checking account is often in the abuser's name alone, or if a joint account, they hold on to the checkbook as though it was their sole possession. Although they demand control over the family finances, they often refuse to pay the bills.

Personal Application:
Describe any patterns of financial abuse that exist in your family:

_____

_____

An alternative form of financial abuse often employed by financial abusers is an extension of childhood "parallel play." This pattern is normally seen in children from age two to five. Children at that age tend to "play together separately." That is, they may be playing on the same blanket or in the same play pen, but each has, and jealously guards, his or her own toys. They share with the other, only when a parent requires them to do so, and then very begrudgingly.

72

Personal Application:
What would "parallel play" look like in marriage?

___

Many couples, have never resolved their childhood issues. Instead, they carry this pattern of parallel play on into marriage and family life. They maintain separate checking accounts, have separate, individually owned cars, have their own books, DVD's, CD's, etc. And, may God help the other person if the other should use any of their possessions!

Personal Application:
Do you and your partner use parallel play?

___

Responsibility Projection - When the abuser employs responsibility projection, he/she tries to make their partner responsible for everything. All the bills, the children's misbehavior, employment problems, problems with extended family and friends, their conflicts, personal problems such as substance abuse, traffic citations, etc. All of these, and much more, are all blamed on the other person. The abuser normally refuses to take responsibility for his/her behavior, and often even attempts to hold his/her partner responsible for their very life, frequently threatening them with statements such as "if (or when) I commit suicide, it will be your fault -- your responsibility -- and then you'll be sorry.")

Personal Application:
Describe patterns of responsibility projection employed by either person in your relationship:

___

Have you, or your partner used the threat of self-harm or suicide?

___

Personal Application:
Why do responsibility abusers have such a difficult time changing?

_____

Responsibility abusers rarely participate in, or complete a counseling or skill-building educational program. After all, their belief is that: "it is after all the other person's fault that I have these problems. Why should I go to counseling, since they are the one who needs help." Mandated participation in an appropriate counseling program, by the court, probation or parole is the best hope for meaningful change in individuals who employ responsibility projection.

Short of this, a skilled counselor can sometimes use the abuser's implicit contract to engage them in the counseling process. An implicit contract is based on what the abuser wants (i.e., "help me stay out of jail," "help me keep my job," "help me keep my husband/wife from leaving"). A skilled therapist can often hook the abuser by convincing him/her that the best way for them to achieve their goal is to enroll, participate in, and complete an appropriate counseling program. When this 'hook' works, and a trusting therapist/abuser relationship is developed, the counselor then has an opportunity to maneuver the abuser from his/her implicit contract, toward the counselor's explicit contract of change,

Substance Abuse - Personal Application:
How can the abuse of psychoactive substances (drugs and alcohol) result in the abuse of one's partner?

_____

_____

_____

Substance abusers often abuse chemicals to anesthetize their own emotional pain, resulting in psychological dependency. Some may have a genetic predisposition to physical dependency, or abuse toxic chemicals over a long enough period of time to develop physical dependency.

In this case, the chemically dependent person will usually require some form of therapeutic intervention to effect a change. In most cases, substance abusers and the chemically dependent will not continue in marriage and family, or any other form of therapy, unless they first address their chemical abuse or dependency.

In families where violence and abuse is a part of the relationship dynamic, chemical dependency may not be the reason for the substance abuse. In this case, there is often an entirely different, more covert, motivation. The substance abuser may abuse, or even feign the abuse of toxic chemicals, as a means of inflicting abuse on his or her partner. Knowing that their partner is vehemently opposed to their use/abuse of such chemicals, they abuse them intentionally as a ploy to demonstrate their power over, and ability to control the other person.

Some intentionally use and/or abuse substances to give themselves permission to express their emotions and inflict abuse and violence while maintaining that they are "not responsible" for what happened, since they were "under the influence." Others use/abuse toxic chemicals to avoid their partner's efforts to resolve conflicts. They go out of their way to convince their partner, that while 'under the influence' they are incapable of resolving conflict.

Personal Application:
Have you used substances to intentionally hurt your partner?

_____

Have you used them to avoid taking responsibility for abuse?

_____

Have you used them to avoid conflict-resolution attempts?

_____

Stalking: Personal Application

Is stalking *really* abuse, or is the person just making sure they can trust their partner?

_____

_____

Stalking is a serious form of abuse. It is a separate crime in most states. Even the federal government, in recognition of the seriousness stalking poses, passed legislation prohibiting stalking and imposing severe consequences for those who do so.

The abuser who employs stalking rarely lets his/her partner out their sight, and even then usually follows them to spy on them, or calls to see if they really are where they said they would be. And upon their return, they interrogate them mercilessly. No place is sacred or private to the victim of a stalker. They will follow their partner to church, to the beautician or barber, the grocery store, their work place, etc. Some won't even let their partner use the rest room with the door closed! Stalkers have a profound inability to trust, are insanely jealous and often threatening (i.e., "If I can't have you, then no one will.")

Personal Application:
How effective is separation or divorce in ending stalking?

There is unquestionably a great deal of stalking that occurs while partners are married or living together, even among those who are engaged or just going steady. But, it doesn't end there. Nor is it limited to partners who are considering separation or are estranged through separation or divorce. Quite the contrary; it often escalates after the couple separates or divorces. Stalking is one of the more serious forms of abuse, often preceding and even predictive of, lethal, even fatal, physical abuse.

We are aware of one case of stalking that ended in a dual fatality. That incident occurred in Denver, Colorado in the early nineties. It involved a pastoral couple -- both ordained ministers. In this case, the husband's insane jealousy and pattern of stalking escalated to the point that his wife no longer felt safe going to church with him. In an effort to avoid further outbursts of his jealousy, she accepted a pastoral position with a different church.

Unfortunately, her best efforts did not stop the stalking. On the contrary, it seemed to escalate it. This woman's husband even changed the schedule of his own church service so he could make certain he was at the church his wife pastored before her service was dismissed -- so he could check on her! One Sunday morning, the wife's church service lasted longer than usual, and tending to her pastoral duties, she took longer than he expected to get out of the church. As his jealous rage mounted, her husband went to his car, put a revolver in his pocket, then resumed his position at the front door of his wife's church, where he impatiently waited for her to exit. When she did, he shot and killed her, then turned the gun on himself and committed suicide. Both pastors fell dead on the church steps!

Personal Application:
Does stalking, of any type, exist in your relationship?

If stalking exists in your relationship, you must take it very, very serious, regardless who the stalker is. Stalking is so serious that most states and the federal government have made stalking a separate, criminal offense. This means that one can not only be charged for stalking, but when domestic abuse and/or violence ensures, stalking, when engaged in, will be counted as an enhancement of the other criminal offense, increasing sentence penalties.

Destruction of Property - Property destruction violence includes a wide array of behavior: behavior such as tearing up photographs and momentos, destroying the other person's clothes and other personal belongings, throwing and breaking dishes and bric-a-brac, throwing things outside, pounding, marring and breaking tables and other furniture, knocking holes in walls, kicking holes in doors and/or breaking doors off hinges, damaging vehicles, abusing pets, etc.

Notably, abusers who employ this form of violence rarely destroy their own things. Most of the property they destroy belongs to the other person or their friends, or belonged to the both of them and is now viewed with contempt. Research statistics indicate that women tend to be responsible for far more single incidents of property destruction; however, when men use this abusive tactic, they destroy property worth many times the value of that property destroyed by women.

For example, I (Jim) am aware of one man who, finding out that his wife had filed for divorce because of his abuse -- but not having yet been served the papers -- hired a bulldozer and demolished their house. His reasoning was, it was community property, he had the *right* to destroy it!

I read of another incident that happened near Seattle, Washington involving a man who thought his wife was cheating on him. One day he was sure he saw her car in front of another man's house he believed to be her lover. In his rage and jealousy, this man ordered a load of ready-mix concrete and had it dumped into his wife's convertible -- on the assumption that since it was *their* car, he could get away with it.

Wrong on both counts! First of all, it turned out to be someone else's car that looked like theirs. Second, his wife was out of town at a business seminar all day and her car was parked at the airport.

One more case that I was personally involved with involved a man who had his property surveyed, and upon discovering that his neighbors garage was partly on his property, took his chain saw and cut the garage in two!. In each case, the judiciary held the property abuser responsible, ordering just restitution!

Personal Application:
Describe any property destruction that has taken place in your relationships:

_____

_____

Physical Abuse: Personal Application:
What is your description of physical abuse?

_____

_____

Most answer this by suggesting that physical abuse involves behavior that results in the injury of the other person (i.e., broken

78

bones, bruises, etc.). However, physical abuse as defined legally, includes any touch or physical contact not given in love, respect and dignity.

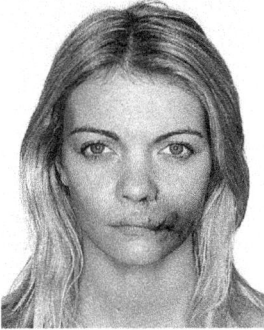

Physical abuse may include any number of the following: pushing, shoving, slapping, pulling hair, grabbing, holding, restraining, pinching, punching, incessantly tickling, slapping, scratching, shaking, kicking, tripping, twisting arms, squeezing or twisting fingers, biting, choking, smothering, punching, hitting, pounding, beating, battering, using weapons, disabling and killing.

Personal Application:
What if one is just trying to keep their partner from hurting them or themselves, or trying to help them regain self-control?

_____

I am personally aware of one case where the husband, when wife came home drunk and began yelling, put a pillow over her face and held her down. His defense in court was that he did it "to keep her from screaming." Nevertheless, he was convicted of assault with a deadly weapon and sentenced to four years in prison. In another case I am familiar with, the deadly weapon involved a flower pot dropped from a second-story window.

Personal Application:
What is domestic violence referred to when both parties are culpable?

_____

Both genders may employ various forms of physical abuse. In fact, reputable research indicates that in "mutual combat," or expressive violence, each gender tends to step into their area of weakness. Men tend to make the first foolish or abusive comments about 70% of the time, while they cannot possibly defend themselves verbally and emotionally against their wife, whose prowess is verbal communication. Women, on the other hand, tend to be responsible for the first physical gesture about 65% of the time, while most are unable to defend themselves in any ensuing physical battle (Neidig & Friedman, 1984).

It should be noted that once physical activity commences, **men inflict approximately 92% of all <u>reported</u> physical injury on**

women. However, this statistic needs clarification to be properly understood. Women, whose flesh has more fat cells than men's tends to bruise far easier than men's. A woman's skeletal structure is finer and more fragile contributing, to their bones breaking more easily than a man's. Another factor that skews this statistic is a well known fact that few men will file a report against their wives, thereby acknowledging that they have been abused and hurt by their female partner.

Personal Application:
Describe briefly, any physical abuse that has occurred in any of your relationships:

_____

_____

_____

_____

Alternative Relationship Dynamics:
There are really only two basic types of family relationship dynamics, or patterns:

Personal Application:
What are these two relationship patterns?

_____

_____

a). There are those families that operate on **The Love of Power**, using the abusive, maladaptive relationship skills we have been discussing.

b:. There are families that operate on a totally different set of principles and practice. These families operate on **The Power of Love**.

Review the "Power of Love Wheel" illustrated on the following page, considering carefully which of the attributes depicted thereon are present, or absent, in your relationships.

The Power of Love:
Families that operate on those *power of love* relationship dynamics illustrated above, demonstrate respect, honor and dignity toward one another. Members of these families respect each other's individual personhood, identity, and reality. These families generally follow the guidelines for a loving relationship delineated

in 1 Corinthians 13, New Testament of the Judeo-Christian Bible. Healthy families adhere to these principles, regardless of their specific spiritual worldview:

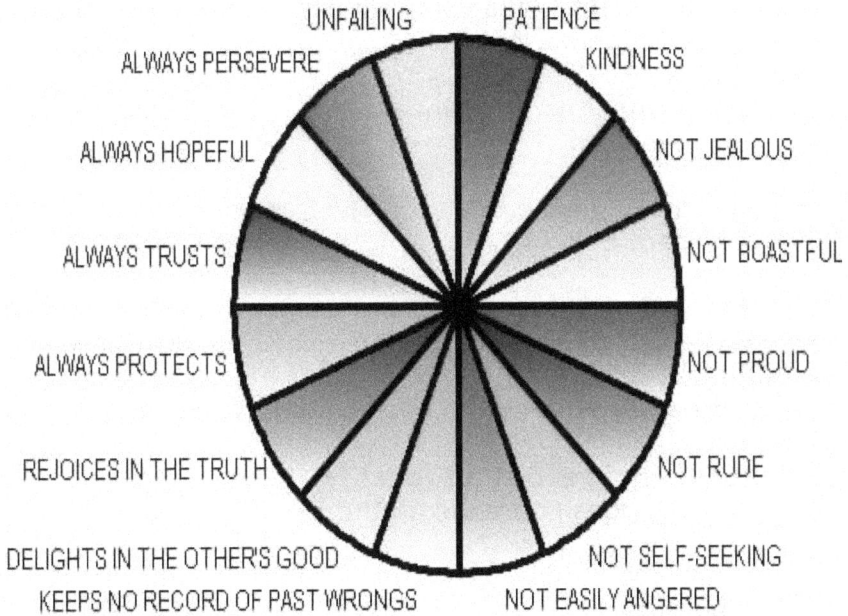

The Power of Love Wheel

"Love is patient, love is kind. It does not envy, it does not boast, it is not proud. It is not rude, it is not self-seeking, it is not easily angered, it keeps no record of wrongs. Love does not delight in evil but rejoices in the truth. It always protects, always trusts, always hopes, always perseveres. Love never fails" (1 Cor: 13:4-8).

THE POWER OF LOVE WHEEL
Compare the qualities depicted on the power of love wheel

depicted on the preceding page, and the descriptions following, with those abusive qualities depicted on the power and control wheel, and described in detail in this chapter:

- **Patience** - forbearance and long-suffering

- **Kindness** - benevolence, grace, or charity

- **not envious** - not covetous, greedy or pathologically jealous

- **not boastful** - not vain, ostentatious, self-righteous, and without grandiosity

- **not proud** - no arrogance, but humble, transparent, open, and teachable

- **not rude** - not crude, abrasive, or vulgar, but gentle and considerate

- **not self-seeking** - not narcissistic, a secure identity and self-worth without an insatiable need for 'atta-boys'

- **not easily angered** - easy going, tolerant, and merciful

- **keeps no record of past wrongs** - present-moment focused, doesn't dredge up the past

- **does not delight in evil** - never laughs at another's misfortune

- **rejoices in the truth** - delights in and celebrates what is, rather than pining for what might be

- **always protects** - defends, secures, shields, and safeguards

- **always trusts** - believes in, relies on, keeps promises, and maintains an open intimate relationship

- **always hopes** - holds positive dreams and fervent aspirations

- **always perseveres** - has a determination to succeed, with no thought of giving up

- **never fails** - love doesn't weaken, fade, decline, or give out over time

Personal Application:
How would you feel about your partner, and your partner about you, if the two of you consistently employed these principles?

_____

Imagine, for a moment, how you would feel about your partner if he/she consistently related to you employing these principles of the power of love. Think how your partner would feel about you if *you* consistently applied these principles in your relationship with him/her! What would your children, friends and extended family members think of you as a couple -- if you both consistently practiced these dynamics in your relationship interaction?

Individual members of families operating on these principles respect each other, celebrate each other's differences and honor one another's individual preferences. These people are rarely experience serious relationship conflict. It is uncommon for them to be found in Family Court, in a domestic violence court or an anger-abatement program.

Personal Application:
Which family dynamic (the power of love, or, the love of power) prevails in your home?

_____

Summary:
Families that operate on the *love of power* relationship dynamics are those that employ the various forms of abusive power and control depicted on the Power and Control Wheel. These families generally have conflictual relationships with unresolved problems between family members, friends, employers, employees, neighbors, etc. They often manifest other dysfunctional patterns as well: patterns such as substance abuse, eating disorders, workaholism, sexual adjustment problems, etc.

Without appropriate and successful intervention, one or more members of these families may easily end up in family court, and/or be referred to an anger-management or chemical dependency program.

Assignment:
Make a concerted effort this week to practice the principles depicted on the "Power of Love" wheel in all your relationship interactions. You may not feel like it, but -- as they say in 12-Step

programs -- "Fake it till you make it!" Apply these principles consistently for one week, regardless of how your partner treats you, and whether or not he/she thinks you insincere. At the end of the week, complete the following survey to evaluate your success.

Personal Follow-up:
After practicing the 'power of love' dynamics for a least a week, do

you feel differently about your partner? _____

If so, in what ways?

_____

How has your partner previously responded to your efforts?

_____

_____

Be Patient.
Don't give up. Remember, you and your family members may have been using many of the destructive power and control techniques for some time. It will take committed practice over a period of time, before these new techniques become a habit and seem natural to you.

GLOSSARY

Abuse - misuse, exploit, mistreatment, mishandle (the misapplication of something that if used correctly would reap positive results).

Ambivalence - the fusion of opposing emotions (i.e., love and hate, fear and aggression) so that they function as one.

Annihilate - eradicate, extinguish, wipe out

Coercion - force, pressure, duress

Conjugal - marital sexual relations

Cunnilingus - oral stimulation of the vagina

Demean - humiliate, cheapen, degrade

Disparage - belittle or talk down to

Dynamics - patterns of interaction

Feign - pretend, fake, put on, counterfeit

Fellatio - oral stimulation of the penis

Filibustering - maintaining an unrelenting verbal barrage, overwhelming the other person, and denying them equal time to express their position

Harangue - ranting and raving

Hypocrondrasis - pretending to be sick

Incest - inappropriate sex between members of a family (i.e., father/daughter, mother/son, brother/ sister, etc.).

Inextricably Intertwined - inseparable, functioning as a single entity

Inflection - tone, accent, volume, pitch, pressure and clarity -- or lack thereof -- of one's voice

Interrogated - questioned, cross-examined--as though on the witness stand in a court

Interjection - intrude, interrupt, enter into uninvited

Maladaptive - misused, dysfunctional

Molestation - inappropriate sex and/or sexual abuse by someone outside one's family

Pedophillia - the sexual abuse of children

Penile penetration - penetration with one's penis

Redirecting - turning away, deflecting, taking a detour

Revilement - railing verbal abuse, vituperation

Scapegoat - one selected to take the blame

Sexualized - awakened sexually

Triangulation - to pull in a third party as an "ally" (i.e., "she said," "they said," and using "we" when no one else is involved)

KEY POINTS

- **Power and Control Wheel**
  Memorize the various types of relationship- destroying abuse patterns depicted on the power and control wheel and make a commitment -- to yourself, your partner, children and others you are in relationship with -- not to use them anymore.

- **Power of Love Wheel**
  Memorize the relationship-building techniques depicted on this wheel and make a commitment to begin using them today.

Opposing Relationship Dynamics

There are only two family relationship dynamic patterns: a) the power of love, and b) the love of power. The power of love builds and enhances relationships while the love of power damages and destroys them. They don't mix.

CHAPTER FOUR
UNDERSTANDING ANGER

Personal Application:
Anger -- just what is it? - Is it an emotion? - A strong emotion? - A compulsion? A primary emotion? A secondary emotion? A reaction? or, what?

_____

What about the nature of anger, is anger good, bad, or neutral?

_____

Anger is described in *Webster's Dictionary* as "a strong *feeling* of displeasure." Synonyms given include wrath, ire, rage, fury, and indignation. Anger has been defined by some as one of man's primary emotions Others define anger as being man's strongest emotion. Still others suggest that it is a secondary emotion; a reaction to other underlying emotions such as frustration, fear, embarrassment, etc. A few authors and researchers have described anger as an involuntary, compulsive reaction.

Anger is, in a sense, all of these; yet in another very real sense, it is none of these. The arousal sensation one experiences when angry is certainly a primary function in mankind. Even very young children experience anger. Anger is, unquestionably, one of the strongest emotional sensations experienced by man. The state of arousal we call anger generates more electrochemical changes within the human body than nearly any other life experience. Anger is also reactive. It can be triggered by many external situations, events and circumstances, and by one's resulting, internal thoughts and emotions.

However, anger does not respond to certain situations and stimuli in the same manner as most emotions. To grasp the significance of this, examine each of the barrels depicted on the following page. As you do, imagine that each barrel holds a certain emotion. One is fear, another sadness, another depression, embarrassment or guilt, etc. Talking with another person about our fear, sadness or depression, embarrassment or guilt, who responds in empathy, warmth and care usually lifts one's spirit, and diminishes the level of fear, sorrow or despondency. In talking out these emotions, one's load, or "container" of that specific emotion is drained, or at least lightened a bit.

Barrels of Emotions

Fear sadness depression Embarrassed guilt   *ANGER*

For example: talking about an embarrassing experience usually dissipates one's feeling of chagrin. Sharing of one's fear with an empathetic listener almost always serves to assuage one's anxiety. Anger, on the other hand, responds in a contrary fashion. The more people one talks to others about their anger, recounting the incident contributing to their anger, the more powerful, the more intense, their anger becomes. Moreover, the more one talks out their anger, the more likely it is that they will act upon it

Personal Application:
Since anger responds so differently, it begs the question: is anger really an emotion? Or, if not an emotion, what is it?

_____

_____

If anger were *really* an emotion, one would logically expect it to respond to "talk therapy" the same as other emotions do. Based on their response, shouldn't anger diminish in power and intensity the more one talks about it? Shouldn't it just disappear after the cause is explained, the way fear or anxiety usually does? The fact that anger does not behave in the same manner as fear, sadness, embarrassment or guilt could be simply that different emotions respond differently; or perhaps, just maybe, anger isn't an emotion at all. But, if not an emotion, then exactly what is anger?

Personal Application:
Whom, or what, can one rely on for an answer to this question?

_____

_____

88

In an earlier lesson we noted that mankind functions in many ways much like a very complex computer or other psycho-cybernetic servomechanism. To understand the workings of a computer or other complex mechanism, the most reliable information is found by talking to its developer, or reading the owners' operational manual he/she developed. No intelligent person would consider purchasing a complex, expensive piece of equipment without securing a copy of the manufacturer's operation and maintenance manual for that specific model. Good owner's manuals always contain a section entitled "technical difficulties," "troubleshooting guide," "frequently asked questions," or some such. Pursuing this comparison, the most reliable answer to the true nature of anger would be found in the words of the inventor, or creator who formed the mechanism that experiences anger.

Fortunately, a detailed operation and maintenance manual is available for this complex psycho-cybernetic servomechanism called "man." We have readily available, a very old, very reliable "Operations and Maintenance Manual" on this fascinating being called "man." This manual provides a great deal of insight into nearly every aspect of man, his life, his relationships, the management of his emotions, his thoughts, his resources, etc. This detailed manual is called the Bible, and It has a lot to say about anger.

For instance, this manual says: *"Everyone should be quick to listen, slow to speak and slow to become angry, for man's anger does not bring about the righteous life that God desires"* (Jas 1:19-20); and, *"In your anger do not sin: do not let the sun go down while you are still angry"* (Eph 4:26).

Personal Application:
Why did the apostle, Paul admonish us not to let the sun go down (or go to bed) when we are still angry?

_____

There are very good, very logical reasons not to "let the sun go down" (or go to bed) while one is still angry." If you go to sleep angry, your subconscious mind will continue to work, attempting to resolve your anger. To do so, your subconscious mind repeatedly processes the activating event contributing to your anger. If your subconscious cannot resolve the problem, it will "stuff it," storing the anger in a subconscious reservoir of unsolved problems.

When this occurs, the chemical changes that took place during the activating event and associated emotional arousal decrease very slowly and often incompletely. These chemical changes, referred to as stress hormones, include increased levels of cortosol, norephinepherine and adrenaline, which were intended to exist at these elevated levels for only very brief periods of time. Their purpose when elevated, is to help one function during times of emergency. Their elevation creates what is called the "fight or flight" response. When this chemical arousal is sustained over long periods of time, these otherwise beneficial hormones can wreak havoc on the human body.

Personal Application:
How serious, *really,* can the effect of one's own elevated hormones be?

Medical science estimates that at least ninety percent (90%) of all physical illness is psychosomatic in nature, That is, it is generated in the psyche (or mind) and somatized (or experienced in the body)]. A fairly recent issue of the American Medical Association Journal stated that medical practitioners estimate that at least ninety percent (90%) of all hospital beds in America are filled due to a single cause: internalized anger and unforgiveness! Wait a minute: Isn't that what the Scripture cited from that old manual said" "In your anger do not sin." Or, as another version renders this text: "*Be angry,* but sin not."

Personal Application:
Is it really possible to be angry -- ***truly angry*** -- and not sin?

Being angry, but sinning not may at first seem like a contradiction. But look at it again: is it a contradiction or a command? It sounds more like an order. To clear up this apparent contradiction, let's look at it in its original context. The Greek text says: "Become exasperated and yet not offend (or miss the mark)." It is indeed a dual command or directive: a) be angry, or exasperated over the injustice; b) and yet sin not (do not miss the mark). Since we are directed both to be exasperated over injustices, but do not miss the mark (or sin); then experiencing anger must not be sin!

Personal Application:
If anger is not a *sin,* then what is it?

To gain a clearer understanding of the true nature anger, it is imperative that we clearly understand what is meant by *sin* in this text. The word used in this text, that is translated as *sin,* is the Greek word 'amartia [harmitia] which literally means to "miss the mark and thus fail to share in the prize."

The Apostle Paul; the biblical author who admonished us to be angry and sin not, also admonished his readers numerous times, to be "just and upright." Most have grown, having been taught, and believing that being *'just and upright'* means to be *perfect*, or without fault, while that *sin* means to be imperfect or morally corrupt. This is not the case.

Harmitia is a Greek word that was commonly used by hunters during the New Testament era. It referred to the distance between the center of the bull's-eye (or center of the target) and the spot where one's arrow pierced the target. That distance was called the *sin.*

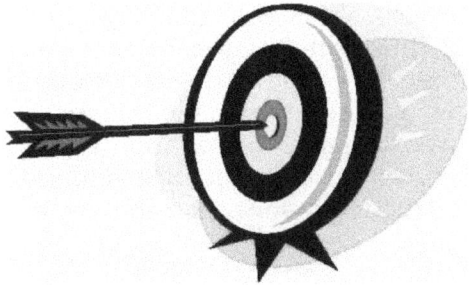

The English term *just and upright,* was translated from one Greek word dikaiw [dikaioo]. This word stems from the same metaphor Paul drew on -- that of an archer. Dikaiw is the word that literally means to "take a careful aim." The Greek hunter or archer, typically got down on one knee, sometimes even bracing himself against a tree or something else, in order to take careful aim.

Taking a careful aim does not ensure that a person will always hit the bull's-eye. Wind, heat-waves, vibration, and any number of things can cause one's best aim to still miss the mark. Above all, hitting the mark (or bull's-eye) requires practice, patience and skill. It takes a strong motivation and courage to succeed. The "mark" Paul is referring to here, is the goal we should all have -- to become a fully realized, fully functional, child of God.

Personal Application:
What does all of this have to do with anger?

Anger properly used helps one achieve the goal of being a fully realized, fully functional, child of God. It fulfills Paul's admonition to sin not, while being just and upright. It also complies with the dual directive to "be angry and sin not." Anger meets these conditions because, rather than being an emotion, anger is a *motivation*. Anger is man's magnificent motivation to succeed, to correct injustice (the missing of the mark). Employed correctly, anger facilitates mankind's renewed attempt to hit the bull's-eye (or reach his goal) of being a functional human being.

ANGER: A Motivation to change. Anger is man's magnificent motivation to correct injustice. Anger is a passion, an almost uncontrollable compulsion to *justify wrongs*, to achieve equity and fairness. What a terrible place our world would be if mankind was not thus motivated to correct injustice. The problem is not that we experience anger, the unfortunate fact is that many do not know how to utilize this magnificent motivation to fulfill its intended purpose. Lacking the appropriate skills to use anger in a manner that will correct injustice and establish equity, we misuse it in a destructive manner, often harming the ones we love the most.

Personal Application:
Why are we so inclined to use anger in a destructive manner?

_____

Many have only seen and experienced anger being misused. Being raised in dysfunctional, maladaptive families, we observed anger being used in an inappropriate manner. We witnessed unskilled models (our parents and other caretakers), unsuccessfully attempt to use anger correctly. To have a compelling motivation to correct injustice, and to attempt to exercise this motivation without adequate skills, is not only ludicrous; it is downright dangerous.

Personal Application:
Are there both good and bad ways to express anger? _____

If so, identify the various ways one might express anger; and describe the differences between them?

_____

_____

_____

_____

There are three basic techniques man uses in his attempts to implement this motivation called anger. They are suppression,

92

repression and expression. These basic methods, and their most probable outcomes, are depicted in the diagram on the following page. Examine the outcome of each of method:

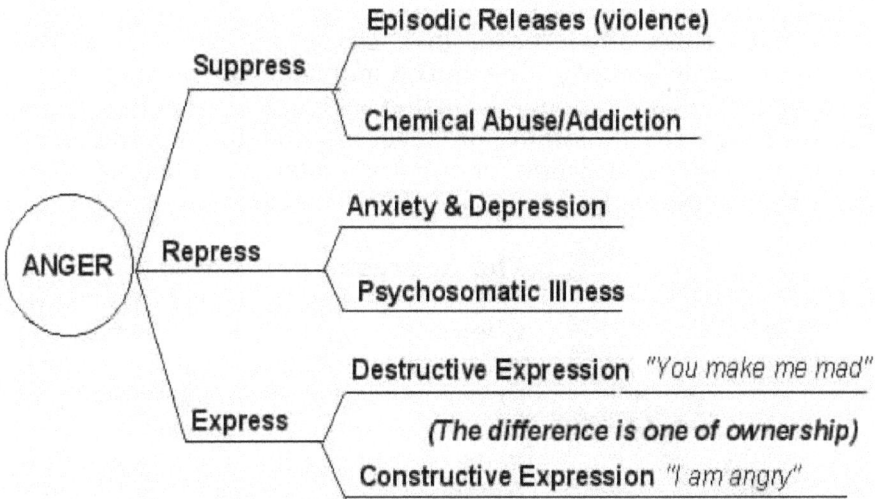

Anger: The Motivation to correct injustice

The Suppression of Anger

The suppression of anger can be likened to building a fire under a boiler and then stopping up the relief valve. After so much pressure is built up, an explosion is inevitable. Suppressed emotions also lead to emotional explosions. These explosions disrupt family harmony, often resulting in damaging others' emotions, physical injuries, and broken relationships. In an attempt to "keep the lid on the pot" as it were, to prevent an explosion, those who suppress their anger often resort to self-medication, abusing alcohol and drugs.

Unfortunately emotional suppression merely covers them up, allowing anger to develop, fester and build. These tactics may keep one's anger from surfacing for a while, but inside the fire is burning, growing in intensity. Then, when it does erupt, somebody suffers -- either another person whom we abuse, or ourselves. The most common form of self-abuse caused by the suppression of anger, is chemical abuse/dependency. This often results in the abuse of others as well, since the chemical abuser manifests his/her anger in an inebriated manner, saying and doing things he/she would never think of in a sober state.

Not only does their anger erupt in a crude and inept way, the abuse of chemicals actually inhibits the individual's ability to "keep the lid on." After each anger arousing incident, it requires more alcohol or drugs to "maintain" or cover up the anger, and each release becomes more crude, inept and volatile, inflicting more pain into the relationship.

The Repression of Anger
The repression of anger happens when the individual becomes so adept at "stuffing it" that they come to believe that they are not angry at all. This is the classical *psychological denial* -- the condition where one has trained themselves not to allow their negative thoughts, feelings and attitudes to surface in their conscious mind. Over time, their denial develops to such an extent they are no longer aware of what is going on within their inner-being -- their deep thoughts, attitudes, emotions and sensations.

When we rely on denial to avoid our negative thoughts, feelings and attitudes, we are actually denying ourselves the basic freedoms of humanity. We can no longer "see what we see," "hear what we hear," "feel what we feel," "perceive what we perceive," "believe what we believe," or "know what we know." We have become disassociated from our own inner-being and have begun living out a false reality.

The outcome of repressed anger is self-abuse, manifest in an unending variety of psychosomatic ills. The most common first indicators are anxiety and depression, but the list goes on and on. Manifestations of repressed anger *can* include:

headaches	migraines	dizziness
hypertension	heart-attacks	heart disease
nightmares	colitis	pancreatitis

94

insomnia	allergies	hives
psoriasis	eczema	skin rash
anxiety	depression	paranoia
panic attacks	arthritis	bursitis
gout	strokes	gastritis
eating disorders	chronic fatigue	stomach aches / ulcers

In other words, anger acted-in against ourselves is just as dangerous, and potentially just as deadly, as when anger is acted-out against another. The primary difference between the two being the identity of the victim (i.e., yourself or the other person).

Personal Application:
Which of these methods of "anger-management" have you most often used and with what results?

_____

_____

The Healthy Alternative: Expressed Anger
The healthy alternative is the expression of anger -- expressing it verbally instead of acting it out (through suppression and the resulting explosions) or acting it in (through repression and denial and the resulting psychosomatic illnesses).

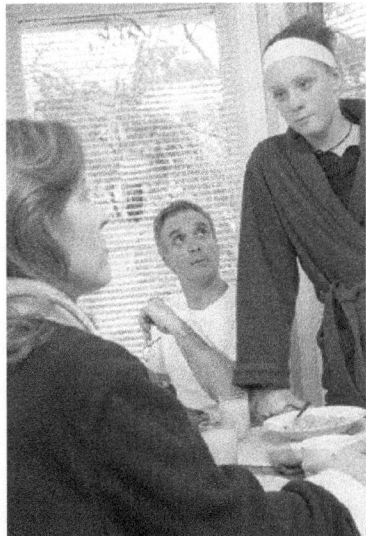

It is also critically important to understand that the expression of anger may be either destructive or constructive. The difference between the two outcomes lies in one thing: one's ownership, or lack thereof, of their anger. More precisely put it has to do with whom _we_ assign the ownership of our anger to. The following examples provide additional clarification:

Destructive expression - The destructive expression of anger involves our assigning the ownership (or cause) of our own anger onto others. This is evident in statements such as: "You make me mad when you . . .," or "I am angry because you did ...," or, "You made me mad when you ...."

Personal Application:
Why is this use of anger so destructive?

_____

_____

The projection of ownership of our anger onto another is destructive for several reasons:

- The other person usually knows, at some level, that the anger is not theirs. Knowing this, they experience a sense of injustice of their own, giving rise to associated negative emotions that can fuel anger. This makes the underlying issue, or initial dispute, doubly hard to resolve.

- Failure to take responsibility for, and ownership of, our own anger, and our projecting it onto the other person, resulting in our "stuffing it." This contributes to our own backlog of unresolved anger. This backlog of anger increases the tendency to behave reactively, vs. Responsively. It simultaneously contributes to the onset of psychosomatic ills, thus diminishing our general health and well-being, including our ability to resolve conflict.

- Anger, when personal ownership is denied, and assigned to another, serves to increase one's tendency to lie to themselves and believe their own lie. This results in multiple misbeliefs and life-commandments that one may operate out of for years. For example: one may tell themselves: "my partner is always angry," and/or "really hates me." This can trigger feelings of rejection, which will fuel anger, that can easily escalate to an episode of violence or abuse. It may even result in the deterioration and/or termination of the relationship. Moreover, it is a lie since the anger was ours all along.

Constructive expression - The constructive expression of anger has to do with one simply taking personal ownership their own anger. This will be evident in thoughts and words such as: "I am angry" or, "I am feeling angry").

Personal Application:
What is the purpose or benefit of my owning my own anger?

_____

_____

- In taking ownership of our anger, we actually empower ourselves. Now that the anger belongs to me personally, I can utilize my own motivation to correct whatever injustice I have just experienced (real or imagined), resolve the underlying negative emotions and release the person or persons I have held responsible for the injustice.

- Taking ownership of our anger does not involve looking outside of ourselves for the cause of our anger. Instead, it guides us to look inside ourselves, to seek insight about the origins of our sense of an injustice and the appropriateness of our associated emotions.

- Often, one will through this insight, discover that their anger has its origins in earlier situations and events involving persons other than the one we now feel angry toward.

- Taking ownership motivates one to release those they have held responsible for injustices experienced. This also frees one from bondage to the other person.

- It advises our partner, child, employer, employee, or other person, that we believe we have suffered an injustice (real or imagined).

- It prevents escalation of the anger and may forestall an episode of violence and/or abuse.

- It protects the other person's emotions and self worth, and finally,

- It avoids harming and may actually save our relationship.

Time Out!
To accomplish this insight normally requires one to temporarily disconnect from the other person. It requires a "time-out."

Personal Application:
What's a time out, and how can this help solve any problem?

_____

_____

A time-out is *not* the same as releasing unmentionable expletives, then walking out and slamming the door. A time-out involves giving yourself the opportunity to learn to recognize when your own or your partner's emotions escalating. It enables one to stop, or interrupt, their interaction before their frustration reaches the point where they act on their compulsion to correct the injustice.

Time-outs are very temporary separations (usually lasting an hour or less), taken for the purpose of allowing one's emotions to settle down and reason to return to both parties. You will notice I said *reason,* not rational or logical thoughts. Logic and rationale involve left-brain cognitions, which are devoid of the right-brain emotional content such as compassion, sensitivity, and empathy. Reason, on the other hand, involves the integration of both cognitive and affective thoughts (usually referred to as thoughts and feelings). Reason infers *saneness, sanity, lucidity, or soundness.*

When one's emotions escalate to the level that they feel compelled to act, to correct the perceived injustice, a process is engaged, *(known as the fight or flight mechanism).* At that point, the person becomes supercharged with adrenaline, cortosol and other associated stress hormones. When this occurs, the person is actually in a different ego-state, or alternate reality.

At this point, one's focus is no longer on the preservation of their relationship. In this altered state of consciousness, our partner (or other person we are engaged with) has become our enemy. Believing this, one feels it is time to run away or "put up their dukes." While in this state of being, our two primary thought processes (our cognitive and effective cognitions) are largely disassociated (or disconnected) from each other.

In this ego-state, experiencing the fight or flight response, one is in the survival mode. When in the survival mode, we will consistently rely on our dominant thought process, tending to ignore the other. Why is this important?

The majority of men (65% to 70%) are left-brain dominant, and rely primarily on their left-hemisphere: cognitive, rational, logical, and judgmental thoughts. The majority of women, on the other hand (70% to 75%), are right-brain dominant, relying primarily on their right-hemisphere affective thoughts: emotions, imaginations, fantasy, etc. Left-brain dominant persons are far more interested in facts and logic, while right-brain dominant individuals are much more interested in everyone's emotions; maintaining the relationship closeness, interdependency and interconnectedness.

Personal Application:
Based on this description, do you think you are left-brain or right-brain dominant?

_____

If you are unsure which thought process dominates, generally triggering your behavior -- whether you give preference to your intellect or emotions -- try the following exercise: put your arms straight out from your body, horizontally to the sides, with the palms of your hands facing inward. Now, close your eyes, and while they are closed, bring your hands together in front of you, clasping them together tightly. Now, open your eyes and see which thumb is underneath, protected by the other. This normally identifies one's thought process dominance.

What, if any, effect does thought process dominance have on one's behavior?

_____

_____

When in a state of significant emotional arousal -- one that involves questions of survival and safety -- the fight or flight syndrome (survival mode) is automatically triggered.

At this time, one's intellectual and emotional thought processes tend to disassociate. When disassociated, we rely on our dominant thought process, largely ignoring the other. In this altered state of consciousness, most men, being left-brain dominant, tend to behave in a manner that _appears_ very reasonable and logical, but devoid of any compassion, empathy or sensitivity. In contrast, most women, being right-brain dominant, tend to behave in what appears to be an _irrational, illogical, emotionally charged_ manner.

In this ego-state, the ability for either to see a situation from the other person's perspective, essential to constructive conflict-resolution, has temporarily flown out the window. Neither party's left and right hemispherical thought processes are integrated. In this ego-state, neither is able to reason. Consequently, they are not reasonable ("reason-able.)" Attempting to resolve conflict and/or correct injustices while in this ego-state is an impossibility. A time out is needed.

Time-outs allow both individuals time to regain their state of reason. To be most effective, *time-outs* should:

- Be taken just as soon as possible -- when either first senses their own, or the other's, emotions escalating,

- Be signaled in a nonverbal manner (i.e., using a hand signal) so there is no further exchange at the moment,

- Last about an hour at first, until both parties' emotions have settled down and they feel calm and re-centered. Over time, the length of time-outs can be reduced as the parties learn better conflict-resolution skills,

- Be taken away from the site of the argument.

Personal Application:
Why is leaving the scene of the argument during a time-out important?

_____

Leaving the site of the conflict during the time-out is critical. Years ago, in the late '70's or early '80's, Bell & Howell Corporation developed a camera that could capture electromagnetic fields on film. With this camera, updated models, still used in police forensic work today, can produce a recognizable photograph, made from a snapshot of a chair where a particular person sat within the preceding twenty-four hours. Imagine the residual energy field!

With this in mind, take into consideration the fact that when angry we have more intellectual, emotional, spiritual and physical energy available than at any other time. We are quite literally *supercharged.* People are, among other things, magnificently complex electromagnetic beings. Every organ, every system of the human body, functions on electrochemical energy. During a conflict, when emotions are high, there is a tremendous amount of electromagnetic energy emitted by both persons.

The site of the conflict has become a powerful energy field. Each party literally "feels" the other's energy. Each person subconsciously knows this energy is emanating from outside themselves. Thus they believe that, the other person is making them mad. Leaving the scene of the conflict allows this energy field to dissipate and one's emotional arousal to subside.

Thus, it is critically important that *both* parties leave the conflict-site for a period of time, usually a minimum of one hour. It is also preferable that the parties select a different place to resume their conflict-resolution efforts after their time-out.

Personal Application:
What is the most important skill you can use to stop family abuse and violence? And, why?

_____

Time-outs are the single most effective tool for stopping family violence and abuse. Time-outs limit emotional escalation; prevent anger from reaching proportions that seem to compel the use of force; and protect the dignity, reality, and self-worth of both individuals. It often protects and preserves the relationship itself. To be fully effective both parties should understand the purpose of, and learn to practice, time-outs. Time-outs save relationships, keep people out of problems with the law, and often save lives.

Time-out CUES:
There are a number of cues, or signs that are manifest, which

suggest that our emotions are escalating to the point that a time-out is necessary. Time-out cues may include the following:

- **Physical changes** such as:
  - Rapid breathing and heart beat
  - Tightness in the chest, neck and/or shoulders
  - Headaches
  - Ringing in the ears
  - Backaches
  - Grinding one's teeth
  - Dry throat and mouth
  - Clinched fists, and/or sweaty palms
  - Impaired digestion and stomach aches
  - Sleep disorders such as insomnia, oversleeping, or fitful sleep
  - Nightmares
  - Agitation and inability to sit still
  - Pacing the floor

- **Emotional changes** such as:
  - Decreased sexual interest or compulsion for sexual satisfaction
  - Feelings of hopelessness, worthlessness, meaninglessness and purposelessness
  - Negativity and cynicism
  - Bitterness and resentment
  - Sadness, fearfulness and depression
  - Unexplained fear, up to and including paranoia
  - Anxiety and panic attacks
  - Forgetfulness, preoccupation and daydreaming
  - Apathy, boredom and chronic fatigue
  - Hatred of those otherwise loved
  - Self-disgust and/or Self-hatred
  - Feeling numb

- **Intellectual changes** such as:
  - Making mathematical and grammatical errors
  - Difficulty articulating words - mispronouncing them
  - Vertigo, or the loss of direction and/or balance
  - Past-oriented: an inability to keep focused on the present moment
  - Decreased creativity and problem-solving capabilities
  - Inability to concentrate
  - Fixated thoughts

- Possible confusion

- **Spiritual changes** such as:
  - Diminished interest in religion and spiritual issues
  - Cessation of reading the Bible or other inspired material
  - Diminished interest in attending church, temple, synagogue, etc.
  - Profound guilt and shame
  - Develops a deep sense of lostness and being unforgivable
  - Angry at God
  - Projecting the cause of one's problems on God, Satan, evil influences, etc.

Take time to identify -- and circle -- those *cues* that can let you, or your partner, know that your emotions are escalating and you are beginning to get angry.

Personal Application:
What are the primary cues that *you* are becoming angry?

_____

_____

_____

After you have identified your anger cues , turn to the ***Time Out Contract*** at the end of this lesson and write these time-out cues in the place provided.

Release TRIGGERS - Triggers are somewhat different from cues. *Triggers* are the signals (behaviors, words, looks, etc.), one's partner needs to recognize in order to head off an impending incident of violence or abuse. They are signs that indicate one's stress has reached the boiling point -- the point at which the fight or flight response is triggered. Recognizing and understanding triggers can provide one's spouse, children and others, warning of an impending release of tension: tension, that if released improperly, could erupt into abuse and violence. When timely recognized and properly understood, triggers can alert an

individual's partner, child or others, to the need for an immediate time-out.

Every human has a limited ability to manage stress constructively. Beyond that, we may all say or do something we will later regret. Identifying and remembering our own time-out cues and each other's release triggers can save a lot of heartache as well as preventing abuse, violence and the fragmentation of one's family unit.

Personal Application:
What are your "triggers" that your partner, children and others. need to be aware of, that signal the urgency for a time-out?

_____

_____

After you have identified the triggers your partner and others should be aware of, write them in the designated place on the *Time Out Contract* at the end of this lesson.

Time-out SIGNALS - A time-out signal is any signal that you and your partner agree on that either of you can give the other when you feel your own emotions escalating, or believe your partner's emotions to be escalating. Time-out signals vary with each couple, but it is best that they be nonverbal to prevent further escalation.

The time-out sign may be the well-known "T" sign made by placing one hand over the top of the other -- the sign one frequently sees at numerous sporting events; or it might be holding up one hand as a caution signal -- frequently used by traffic policemen; or any other nonverbal signal you both can agree on.

Personal Application:
What time-out signal will you and your partner use?

_____

_____

Duration of Time-out - The duration of time-outs must be based on the length of time required for both persons' emotions to settle down. This varies greatly from person to person. Introverts (or loners) usually require far more time for their emotions to settle down than extroverts (socialites).

A time-out of sixty minutes (one hour) is usually a good place to start. After personal experimentation, the time-out period can be lengthened or shortened to fit you and your partner's individual personalities. Remember, however, that your time-outs need to be long enough for *both* parties' emotions to settle down. If your emotions settle down sooner than your partner's, be sure to allow him/her sufficient time to achieve the same results that you obtain in a lesser time, or if you take longer to become calm and serene, allow yourself the necessary time before trying to re-engage.

Keep in mind, that should one of you leave the residence during a time-out, it is always a good practice to call home before returning. This will enable you to determine whether or not the other person has had sufficient time for their emotions to settle. If not, calling before you return home, will let you know it is best to wait a bit longer before going home. This practice can help prevent a continuation, or resumption, of the same, unresolved conflict.

Personal Application:
How long do you feel that your and your partner's initial time-outs should be to allow both you and your partner to calm down?

_____

What are some of the things one can do during time-outs that will help a person calm down?

_____

Time-out Activities - During your time-outs, try taking a walk, getting some exercise, reading a book or listening to calming music. Meditate, pray, or whatever most helps *you* calm down.

Personal Application:
What are some things one should not do during time-outs, and why?

_____

_____

Time-out Rules - During time-outs, it is important to avoid using any alcohol or drugs, or driving. The use of alcohol or drugs lowers a person's inhibitions, impairs judgment-making abilities, and elevates one's emotions. Any or all of these effects can lead to a resumption of conflict and increase the potential for abuse and/or violence.

Driving during a time-out is not advisable since one's emotional state is already unstable. A person is far more accident-prone during periods of emotional instability and high anger. You may also want to avoid eating during an anger episode. Many individuals tend to eat when upset, thinking this will help calm their emotions. However, the increased level of stress hormones caused by anger can result in overeating and indigestion.

Finally, a word to pregnant and nursing mothers. If pregnant, remember that your unborn child is connected to you through the umbilical cord. The ingestion of alcohol, or the use of drugs, results in these substances being passed on to your unborn child. Moreover, since the umbilical cord connection gives preference to the unborn, the level of nutrients, or toxic chemicals, in the unborn child's blood stream will be approximately fifteen percent (15%) higher than in the mother's. This is true also of the stress hormones generated during an episode of anger. The increase in the mother's stress hormones will be transmitted directly to her baby.

If you are a nursing mother, you should know that any toxic substance ingested, inhaled, or injected, will be passed to the infant through the mother's milk. Since the unborn or infant child's central nervous system (CNS) is still rapidly developing, they are far more susceptible to the negative effects of these chemical overloads.

Laboratory researchers have, for decades, used Guinea Pigs to test the potential effects of medicines and other chemicals on humans since a Guinea Pig's blood chemistry is much like that of a human. Researchers have found that a very small amount of blood, taken from an angry person and injected into the Guinea Pig, will result in its death! This is caused by a lethal overload of stress hormones. In unborn and infant babies, these effects can be just as disastrous. There are documented cases of a woman becoming enraged while nursing her baby, and having her infant die in her arms -- from a lethal does of the stress hormone, cortosol! One can only conjecture how many 'spontaneous' abortions have been caused from a toxic overload of their mother's stress hormones.

Personal Application:
What can my partner and I do at the end of a time-out to prevent a continuation of the argument?

_____

_____

Time-out Termination

After checking in with the other party to see if they are ready to terminate the time-out, the reunion should begin by both parties affirming one another for taking the appropriate step (a time-out) to help prevent an episode of violence or abuse. Following this time of mutual affirmation, set an appointment, by mutual agreement. It should be fairly soon, so neither party things they are just being put off. Moreover, if too far distant, memories concerning the original conflict and its antecedents will fade. BE certain to keep this appointment, and when the two of you meet to resume your conflict-resolution efforts, limit your dialogue and resolution efforts to the issue that led up to your time-out.

Personal Application:

Why set an appointment? Shouldn't my partner and I attempt to solve the issue that resulted in our argument as soon as possible?

_____

Never try to re-engage immediately on your return. Wait until you are both better centered and have had adequate time to analyze your own position -- your thoughts, emotions, attitudes, beliefs and expectations. Failing to allow one another this time most often results in a resumption of the conflict, since we all tend to be defensive when we feel hurried or pressured.

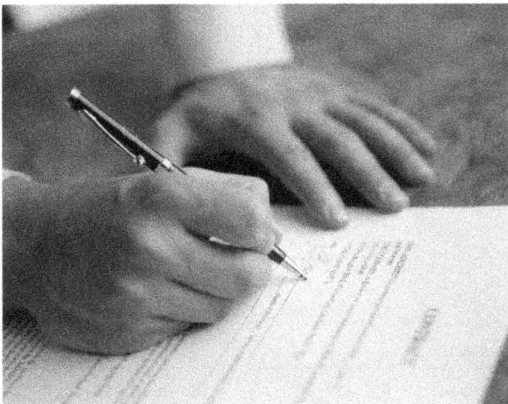

Time-out Contract - Take a few minutes to fill out the _Time-out Contract_ on the following page. Then, take time to share this contract with your partner and make a covenant with him or her that you will employ the time-out skill to prevent future violence and abuse. Ask their cooperation in honoring time-outs, but, _don't_ demand it.

TIME-OUT CONTRACT

Time-outs are one of the most successful interventions in domestic violence and abuse. Moreover, it is a technique available to you *immediately*. TIME-OUTS are a brief separation of an hour or so, designed to allow both parties time for their emotions to calm down. Time-outs are to be used when you feel your emotions rising or when you observe your partner's anger "cues."

The cues that I am getting angry are:

_____

_____

_____

The "triggers" (red flags) my partner needs to know are:

_____

_____

The neutral, non-blaming time-out signal that "I" will use will be:

_____

When "I" give this signal, "I" will say:

"I'm getting angry" and then leave the scene without blaming.

When I leave, I will go ... (where)?

_____

When my partner gives the time-out signal, "I" will allow her/him to leave, honoring their request for a time-out.

The time-out will last for _____ minutes.

During the time-out, "I" will _____

_____

At the end of the time-out, my partner and I will:

_____

Acknowledgments

Self   _____   _____

Partner   _____   _____

Time-out Practice - No new skill or technique feels particularly comfortable when one first begins to use it. In fact, most new behavioral patterns initially feel uncomfortable, or at least a bit awkward. Like any new skill, it is important that a couple keep practicing their time-outs, until they both feel comfortable. To develop this habit, begin by taking practice time-outs, preferably when they are not *really* needed. This will increase your comfort in the process and make it more likely that you will rely on this technique when the need arises.

Remember, "Practice makes perfect."

GLOSSARY

Anger - mankind's magnificent motivation to correct injustice

Chagrin - embarrassment, confusion

Compulsion - a behavior that seems to be driven by something out of our control

Cue - clue, hint, suggestion, sign

Diminish - reduce, shrink, lessen

Disassociated - disconnected, having little or no internal association between our thoughts and feelings about an incident

Dissipate - dissolve, fade, melt away

Dysfunctional - to function abnormally or improperly

Escalating - rising, increasing, mounting

Expression - to voice, utter, verbalize, gesture

Inept - unskillful, unsuitable, improper

Maladaptive - inadequate or faulty adaptation of something that results in defeating its intended purpose

Motivation - inspiration, stimulation, impetus, encouragement

Psychocybernetic - man's goal-oriented mind

Psychosomatic - related to the mind-body connection, physical states of being produced by our thought processes

Reason - lucidity, sanity, soundness, saneness

Repression - to push below the level of one's consciousness

Servomechanism - a direction, or goal-correction device

Sin - to miss the mark -- failing to be who we are (a child of God) [In early Greek times the "sin" was the distance from the center of the bulls-eye of a target to the point the arrow entered

Suppression - to hold back, choke, stifle, squelch

Time-out - a break, intermission, recess after which time one resumes an appropriate activity

Trigger - a stimulus that provokes to action

Volatile - temperamental, unstable, unpredictable

KEY POINTS

- **Understanding Anger as a motivation**

- **The three methods of dealing with anger:**
    - Suppression
    - Repression
    - Expression

- **The two type of expressed anger:**
    - destructive
    - constructive
    Know the difference (ownership)

- **The results of suppressed anger:**
    - explosive, violent releases
    - addictions

- **The results of repressed anger:**
    - anxiety and depression
    - psychosomatic illness

- **Understand "Psychological Denial"**

- **Know the purpose for Time-out**

- **Know the cues you express when angry**

- **Know what triggers you**

- **Understand why it's important to leave the scene of an argument**

- **Understand *Time-out Signals*, *Time-out Period*, *Time-out Activities* and *Time-out Rules***

- **Complete and return your Time-out Contract**

CHAPTER 5
BENEATH THE ANGER
UNDERSTANDING EMOTIONS

Review:
In the last chapter, we learned that anger is a positive force -- a magnificent motivation for good -- when used correctly, to correct injustice and restore equity. We also learned that we have a higher level of energy when angry than during any other emotional state. We also saw that the execution of this motivation, we call anger, can be very ruinous unless it is carried out by employing constructive conflict-resolution skills. Finally, you were introduced to one of the primary conflict-resolution tools, that of "time-out's."

Reflect on your efforts to incorporate this skill. How well did you do? And, how well did your time-outs work?

Taking Our Emotional Temperature
Learning to take our emotional temperature -- to look beneath our anger and discover the nature and intensity of our true emotions -- is the second most important anger-management and conflict-resolution skill.

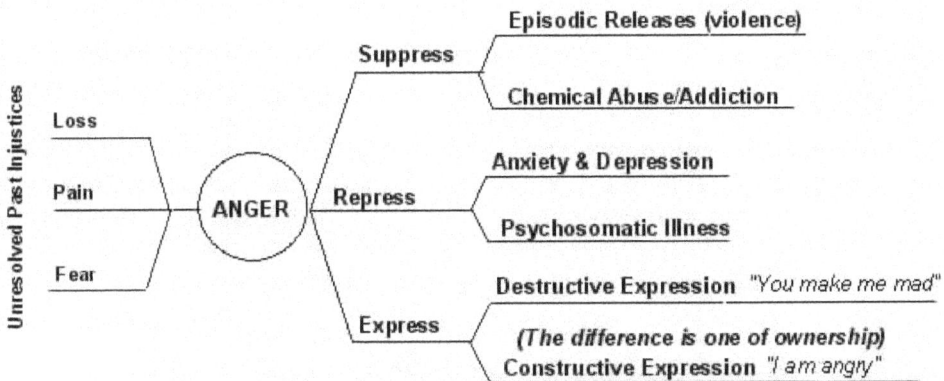

Anger: The Motivation to correct injustice

To understand the application of this skill or tool, review the preceding diagram, depicting the three methods of using anger, that was introduced in the last lesson. In this lesson, we have added to this diagram, identifying those things giving rise to anger, depicted to the left of the circle inscribed, "Anger." This provides a more complete picture of the nature and purpose of anger. Beneath one's anger are our *real* emotions; negative emotions that call forth anger: the God-given motivation to correct injustice.

Every time we suffer an inequity -- real or imagined -- we experience a sense of injustice or loss, whether minor, moderate, significant or disabling. In addition to real losses -- such as the loss of a loved one in death, the loss of a car that was stolen, etc., we interpret unrealized expectations as losses. The losses experienced through unrealized expectations may be as mild and transient as misplacing our car keys, causing us to fear missing an appointment, losing an argument or not getting our way; or as severe as learning that a loved one has just been diagnosed with a fatal illness. In each case, our 'loss' is based on expectation rather than experience.

Loss & Pain

Whatever the injustice, whatever the loss, that we experience or believe we will experience, we automatically meet with a negative emotional arousal -- some form of emotional pain. The nature and severity of one's emotional pain depends on the gravity of the loss itself, and one's own interpretation of that loss (e.g., its personal impact). The degree of impact of any loss depends on two things: a) our level of attachment to what or who we have lost; and b) our perception of the permanence of that loss.

Remember, *emotions* are "energy-in-motion." Emotions are, in reality, biochemical, or electrochemical, messengers providing one information or data: data about their own body and their immediate environment. The particular emotion or emotions we experience depend on the locus (location) of the biochemical arousal or change, our realization of the loss or unrealized expectation, and our personal interpretation of the transient or permanent nature of that loss.

Pain

In other words, our interpretation of any loss depends on the value we assign to the object or person lost, or believed lost; as well as our belief about the permanence of that loss. For example: losing the keys to our car certainly elicits some negative emotions. However, the impact is not nearly the same as if we lost the car itself. Falling down and losing a piece of skin will certainly cause pain, but not the same amount, either physically or emotionally, as if we lost a finger or an arm. Losing a distant relative may cause some pain, but not the same level of pain as if we lost, in death, one emotionally dear to us, such as a parent, child or spouse.

The source, locus, or location of emotions varies as well. These varied sources are depicted in the following chart of emotions, adapted from the *Stevens Ministry* manual.

Severity of Pain
The severity of pain associated with these varying losses is relative to both the value we placed on the object or person lost and our belief about the permanence of the loss. Imagine the difference you would experience emotionally, if you can't locate your car keys and believe that: a) you have just misplaced them and they will soon show up, as compared to b) believing that someone stole them so that they might later come back, steal your car and perhaps invade your home.

Imagine if possible, that you have just lost a loved one in death. Now, regardless which philosophy concerning death and the hereafter that you personally subscribe to, envision the difference level of emotions you would experience between: a) believing that this is the *end* (that you will never, never see that person again), or b) that there is an afterlife, and you will meet your loved one again.

Fear
The uncertainty, the question of resolution (the when and/or whether, or not, the lost will be restored to us), is the *fear* depicted in the diagram on the preceding page. First comes the sense of loss, followed by the ensuing emotional pain as the reality of that loss sinks in, which results in triggering fear -- fear that there may be no resolution -- that the injustice cannot be rectified.

Personal Application:
Why do I fear some things more than others?

_____

_____

_____

The level of fear we experience is, like our other emotions, dependent on our own personal belief systems. The more we tend to believe that there is no resolution, no possible hope for rectifying the injustice, the greater our fear.

Personal Application:
Sometimes we may feel that our fear will destroy us. How serious is fear?

Locus of

Physically Oriented Emotions		Ego-State Oriented Emotions		Cognitively Oriented Emotions	
alert	listless	afraid	grieved	absorbed	interested
	nervous	aggravated	happy	alert	intrigued
aroused	refreshed	agitated	horrified	amazed	involved
beat	relaxed	alarmed	hurt	ambivalent	optimistic
breathless	restless	amused	infuriated	complacent	perplexed
cold	run-down	angry	irked	composed	puzzled
comfortable	rushed	annoyed	irritated	concerned	reluctant
energetic	shaky	anxious	jealous	confused	skeptical
enervated	sick	apprehensive	jittery	engrossed	stimulated
enlivened	steady	astonished	joyous	fascinated	unconcerned
exhausted	stiff	bad	jubilant	hesitant	uninterested
exhilarated	strong	bitter	lonely	inquisitive	unnerved
famished	tense	calm	mad		
fat	tired	comfortable	melancholy		
fatigued	titillated	concerned	merry		
full	uncomfortable	confused	miserable		
gorged	unsteady	contented	mortified		
hot	warm	cross	needed		
hungry	weak	dejected	nettled		
hurt	weary	delighted	overjoyed		
ill	well	depressed	pleased		
invigorated	wide-awake	disappointed	rancorous		
jittery	worn	discouraged	relieved		
lethargic		disgruntled	resentful		
		disgusted	sad		
		dismayed	scared		
		displeased	shocked		
		distressed	sorrowful		
		distraught	spellbound		
		disturbed	splendid		
		downcast	surprised		
		downhearted	taken-aback		
		ecstatic	tense		
		elated	terrified		
		electrified	touched		
		embarrassed	tranquil		
		enthralled	troubled		
		exhilarated	undone		
		frightened	uneasy		
		frustrated	unhappy		
		furious	upset		
		glad	vexed		

One can actually become immobilized through fear. This state of emotional immobilization is referred to as catatonic paranoia. This is paranoia (or fear) so great that it literally puts one in a catatonic state -- a state in which we disassociate from our emotions, our intelligence shuts down, and our body is immobilized. To better comprehend this, consider the following actual example.

Emotions

Spiritually Oriented Emotions		Slang Words used to Describe Emotions	
alive	indifferent	beat	pooped
apathetic	insecure	blahs	psyched out
awakened	inspired	blue	psyched up
bad	joyful	brokenhearted	run-down
bored	joyous	burned-out	rushed
bound	jubilant	charged	shot
committed	lonely	down	spent
complacent	lost	edgy	teed-off
confident	loving	electrified	ticked-off
dead	optimistic	grossed	together
defeated	overwhelmed	groovy	turned-off
despaired	peaceful	hacked off	turned-on
detached	penitent	heaped up	under the weather
discouraged	pessimistic	high	undone
disheartened	powerful	horny	unglued
dissatisfied	powerless	hot	unhinged
downhearted	proud	in-touch	up
dying	redeemed	keyed-up	uptight
empty	renewed	loose	wasted
enlightened	repentant	mellow	whipped
enlivened	satisfied	messed up	wiped
fearful	secure	miffed	wiped-out
free	shamed	mope	wired
fulfilled	strong	off	with it
full	sure	on	wound tight
good	thankful	on-edge	Wound up
guilty	touched	out of it	whipped
helpless	trustful	out of touch	zapped
hopeful	unsure		zonked
hopeless	whole		
	alive		

117

One Saturday afternoon, I received a call from one of my clients' family, pleading for me to come to their home to help them deal with an emergency. Their grandson, and my client, had been experiencing deep emotional pain over an early life experience of having been sodomized by his uncle. He had come to believe that there was something dreadfully wrong with himself, or the abuse would never have happened. He even feared that as a result of that experience, he would eventually lose his masculinity.

After divulging this experience, and his fear, to me in counseling the previous Thursday afternoon, he left my office. Shortly after arriving home, as he reflected on having divulged his "secret" he became overcome with fear -- fear that emanated from his own misbelief. To "protect" himself from his paranoia, he had locked himself in the bathroom and had since, refused to come out.

He had, I learned, used this "technique" several times before, in order to isolate himself from his family. Since it had happened before, his grandparents, whom he lived with, thought little about it. However, when he refused to come out all night long and throughout the following day, they became concerned. By Saturday afternoon, their concern escalated to desperation and they called my office, to request my assistance. They explained that they had been trying in vain for nearly two days to coax him out of the bathroom, all to no avail. They said that they could hear him breathing, but could not get him to respond to anyone or anything.

When I reached their home, I tried all the tricks of the trade to coax him out of the bathroom. Attempting to elicit a response from him, I tried persuading, confronting and challenging -- but got absolutely no response. Lastly, I asked for a clothes-hanger. Straightening the hanger out, I picked the lock and opened the door. There in the middle of the room stood my client, stiff as a statute. He was poised on one foot, one hand on the adjacent lavatory counter, in a profound catatonic state! He was stiff as a corpse and wide-eyed, staring vacantly out the only window in the room.

He had obviously been in that position for many hours, during which, he had even lost control of his bodily functions. Dried Mucous covered his face. He had urinated and defecated in his clothing! I tried repeatedly to awaken him, talking, shouting and even mildly shaking him -- without avail. Accomplishing nothing, I called 911 for help. When the medical rescue team arrived, it required an injection of double dose of a powerful sedative just to get him to relax enough to seat him in a wheelchair to transport him to the hospital -- all because of his fear!

Personal Application:
What things are you most fearful of are?

_____

_____

FEAR [False Evidence Appearing Real]
Nothing had happened to the young man described in the example given: nothing immediately preceding his state of catatonia, at least. He was, instead, reacting to his own fear: fear based on a misbelief that an old, unresolved injustice had intolerable, irreconcilable consequences. What a perfect example of fear functioning as stated in the following well known acronym:

False

Evidence

Appearing

Real

Personal Application:
Can I, or should I, trust my emotions? _____

Explain your answer:

_____

_____

Is it true that situations, events and circumstances we encounter, and/or the actions or inaction's of others create our emotions (cause us to feel a certain way)?

_____

Explain your answer:

_____

_____

The Truth About EMOTIONS

Emotions don't "just happen." Events, circumstances and situations "just happen," but emotions are created. They are our very own creation, based on our individual and unique perception of an event, circumstance or situation: a perception that we create by filtering our sensory information (what we see, hear, smell, taste and touch(through our very own personal beliefs. Relying on this filter, we create our own interpretation.

No two people subjected to a common event share the exact same emotion. Each person's unique perceptual senses vary in type and intensity. For example, I am a bit colorblind. When I look at the color-perception charts, I see a different number embedded within the varied colored dots than most people do -- sufficiently different it prevented me from entering electronics training in the Navy. Many wear healing aids to accommodate for auditory deficiencies, etc. Thus, each and every person's experience of the same event will vary.

Think back to the last time you went to a movie theater to watch a dramatic movie such as "Titanic," "Earthquake," "Tornado," etc. If it's been a while since you viewed such a movie, take a moment the next time you go to such a movie, and watch the people in attendance rather than focusing on the movie. The first thing you will notice is that they all seem to be watching the same scenes on the screen. However, if you look closer, you may notice that the emotions expressed in their faces differs widely. One may be expressing anger, another fear, another sadness, another humor and still another boredom.

Their varying emotions are all exhibited in response to the same scene. Obviously then, it is not the scene on the screen that is creating their emotions. It is their individual perceptions, beliefs and interpretations of a particular scene. In addition to a wide variation of specific emotions felt, the intensity of their emotions may vary tremendously. Some may be experiencing a mild emotional arousal, others a moderate arousal, and still others a substantial, severe or near disabling emotional arousal.

Understanding Emotions

The varied source (location, or locus) of emotions depicted in the previous "Locus of Emotions" chart, adapted from *Steven's Ministry,* and the varying levels, or intensity, of emotions, as depicted on the following "Emotional Vocabulary" chart, demonstrate the widely varying emotional experience individuals might undergo when exposed to external stimuli.

120

The lower one can learn to "catch," or become aware of, their emotions, the greater one's ability to manage them properly. Conversely, the greater the intensity of our emotions before we become aware of them, the more difficult it is to intervene, or interrupt them, and deal reasonably with the activating situation, circumstance or event. Unfortunately, many individuals have lost the ability to apprehend and understand their emotions until they have escalated to the severe range.

EMOTIONS: Can You Trust Them?

Childhood abuse, abandonment or traumatization, including one growing up in a troubled family where he/she could not be themselves, usually results in *emotional disassociation*. We learned as children to disassociate (disconnect) our thoughts and feelings in order to survive chaotic situations. Adults often report having survived profound emotional chaos by 'pretending' that they were somewhere else at the time. As children this helps us survive, but once this defense mechanism is established, a person is inclined to rely on disassociation whenever subjected to stressful, confusing situations.

It is impossible to selectively disassociate: choosing to feel certain emotions and not others. Therefore, when children who relied on disassociation to deal with stress become adults, whenever they people experience an arousal of negative emotions, they disassociate or distance themselves from their emotions to survive. In so doing, they become less and less aware of their emotional life. Over time they become insulated from all but the most intense emotions, preventing them from attending to milder, more manageable, emotional arousal.

Moreover, because one's more severe emotions are usually associated with survival issues, they trigger our automatic 'flight or fight' response. The a result being, that person tends to overreact to situations, usually inappropriately, often violently.

To grasp this, imagine standing on a bridge, believing you are 'protected' from whatever is happening beneath the deck. This is how a disassociated person tends to lives his or her life -- on the deck of a bridge, wholly unaware that the vast majority of their emotional life is taking place beneath the structure. Unaware of those emotions, they deal only with those emotions intense enough to pierce the deck of the bridge, causing damage. Then, believing that all emotions are destructive, they build even stronger defense mechanisms to insulate themselves from their emotions.

	happy	caring	depressed	inadequate	fearful
INTENSE	thrilled	martyr	despondent	worthless	terrified
	on cloud 9	captivated	desolate	like nothing	horrified
	euphoric	codependent	dejected	washed up	desperate
	elated	devoted	hopeless	powerless	panicky
	ecstatic	adoration	alienated	helpless	terror
STRONG	excited	loving	despair	crippled	stage fright
	sensational	infatuation	gloomy	inferior	dread
	exhilarated	enamored	dismal	impatient	vulnerable
	fantastic	cherish	bleak	emasculated	paralyzed
	terrific	affection	empty	useless	immobilized
	top of world	idolize	barren	finished	anxiety
	turned on	worship	grieved	a failure	
	enthused		grim	a nobody	
	delighted				
	marvelous				
	great				
MODERATELY-STRONG	cheerful	caring	distressed	inadequate	afraid
	lighthearted	affirming	upset	whipped	scared
	happy	fond of	downcast	defeated	fearful
	serene	high regard	sorrowful	incompetent	apprehensive
	wonderful	respectful	demoralized	inept	jumpy
	high spirits	admiration	discouraged	overwhelmed	shaky
	up beat	concern for	miserable	ineffective	threatened
	aglow	hold dear	pessimistic	deficient	distrustful
	glowing	prize	tearful	lacking	at risk
	jovial	cherish	weepy	incapable	alarmed
	elated	honor	rotten	insignificant	butterflies
	riding high	taken with	horrible	unimportant	awkward
	cool	turned on	terrible	incomplete	defensive
	neat			no good	unstable
				unfit	chicken skin
					goose bumps
MODERATE	joyful	trusting	melancholy	less-than	anxious
	gratified	close	blue	inefficient	nervous
	glad		lost	small	worried
	contented		unhappy		on-edge
	pleased		down		self-conscious
			blahs		
			glum		
MILD	good	warm	bad	no-confidence	hesitant
	satisfied	friendly	low	unsure	timid
	pleasant	positive	sad	uncertain	shy
	pleased	cordial	disappointed	weak	uneasy
	fine	like			bashful
	calm				ill-at-ease
	normal				doubtful
					uncomfortable

Vocabulary

confused	hurt	angry	lonely	guilty
bewildered	destroyed	furious	abandoned	shamed
baffled	crushed	enraged	rejected	unforgivable
confounded	ruined	seething	isolated	humiliated
perplexed	degraded	infuriated	neglected	disgraced
puzzled	demeaned	outraged	forsaken	heart sick
	disgraced	fighting mad	cut off	mortified
in a dilemma	wounded	pissed off		naked
befuddled	pained	violent	unloved	exposed
in a quandary	devastated	abusive	unwanted	ashamed
confused	injured	indignant	separated	grieved
interrogated	humiliated	bitterness	detached	remorseful
questioning	anguished	resentful	ignored	
	at mercy of	hatred		
	cast away	vengeful		
	forsaken	galled		
	discarded	viscous		
	dejected	nauseated		
mixed up	hurt	irritated	lonely	guilty
disorganized	belittled	hostile	alienated	crummy
foggy	shot-down	annoyed	estranged	upset
troubled	overlooked	frustrated	remote	to-blame
adrift	abused	upset-with	alone	lost-face
awash	depreciated	agitated	separated	demeaned
lost	demeaned	mad	insulated	
at wits end	criticized	aggravated	transparent	
in a cloud	defamed	offended		
circling	censured	antagonized		
disconnected	discredited	exasperated		
disassociated	disparaged	belligerent		
flustered	laughed-at	mean		
in a bind	maligned	vexed		
ambivalent	mistreated	spiteful		
embroiled	ridiculed	vindictive		
disturbed	devalued	disgusted	excluded	regretful
helpless	scorned	turned-off	lonesome	embarrassed
distraught	mocked	teed-off	aloof	wrong
	scoffed-at	irked		lamenting
	exploited	cross		
	slandered			
	defamed			
	impugned			
	slammed			
uncertain	put-down	uptight	left-out	at fault
unsure	neglected	disgusted	excluded	in error
uncomfortable	overlooked	bugged	distant	responsible
undecided	minimized	miffed	unnoticed	blew-it
	letdown	perturbed		goofed-up
	unappreciated	chagrined		
	Taken for granted	dismayed		
		impatient		

Each of the primary emotions listed at the top of the columns in the preceding table, can be sensed in varying degrees of intensity, as depicted by the vertical scale. Learning to get in touch with our emotions in the mild to moderate range will keep them from escalating and becoming so intense that we find it difficult not to act them out.

It feels safe to stay out of that pool of emotions down there below the bridge. It is so much more "calm" on the bridge than in the troubled water below. Gradually, almost imperceptibly, one decides to not even think about what is happening "down there." Unfortunately, what is happening "down there" -- below the level of one's conscious awareness (in one's subconscious mind) can be devastating.

If we are no longer in touch with -- no longer sensing -- our *real* emotions, we may begin to interpret our anger (the magnificent **motivation** to correct injustice) as *the* **emotion**. Denied the right of spontaneous expression, our emotional life becomes distorted, convoluted and dwarfed. Over time, our emotions become impaired, ceasing to mature. The result is, we become ***developmentally arrested***, unable to feel our full range of emotions and attend, or respond, to them. Developmentally arrested, we continue to mature physically, and may intellectually function within the normal range, but we are arrested (or handicapped) in our emotional, motivational and developmental maturity.

When an individual is *developmentally arrested* it means his/her emotional age and developmental abilities have ceased to mature while they continue to grow and age physically! Thus, when called into action, by their fight or flight response mechanism, they behave in a manner fitting for a much younger person, but totally inappropriate for an adult.

Personal Application:
How can one tell if he or she is developmentally arrested?

_____

_____

_____

Signs of Arrested Development:
The following symptoms, when manifest in one's life on a regular, or consistent basis -- particularly when one is experiencing stress or strong emotions -- are manifestations of arrested development.

- adolescent egocentricity - having a self-focus and a simultaneous inability to see life, or gain understanding about a situation from another person's perspective.

- lack of creativity with concrete thinking - a kind of polarized, black/white, perfect/terrible wonderful/throw-it-out type of thought process.

- inability to adequately solve problems dealing with everyday life situations -- particularly relationship issues.

- obstinate/defiant behavior - making sure we do not do what is expected or desired of us, or finding an alternative way of doing what we have been directed to do, rather than carry out the plan given us.

- temper tantrums - reenacting the "terrible-twos" (e.g., stomping our feet, pounding walls, yelling and screaming, etc.).

- infantile behavior - such as curling up in a fetal position, thumb-sucking, bedwetting, or hiding.

- codependency, addictions and other life-controlling problems - substance abuse, sexual addiction, pornography addiction, promiscuity, etc.

- poor and/or unhealthy personal boundaries - an inability to say no,

- Legalistic, having overly rigid boundaries.

- obsessive/compulsive behavior patterns - including many forms of "driven-ness" (i.e., workaholism, shopaholism, compulsive gambling, etc.).

- responsibility issues - believing that we are responsible for other's behavior, or they are responsible for ours.

- power and control issues -- attempting to gain or restore self-control by exercising control over our environment and everyone in it, often resulting in domestic or family violence.

Personal Application:

Which of these signs are evident in your life?

_____

_____

_____

How can one break out of the bondage of arrested development and mature?

_____

_____

Breaking the bondage of arrested development demands that we "make friends" with our emotions and resolve past injustices -- real or imagined. To do this, we must first become aware of our buried emotions, allow them to surface, attend to them and then take time to understand them.

Personal Application:
What's the problem with being emotionally disassociated and arrested?

_____

_____

Persons who are developmentally arrested frequently misinterpret their own emotions. For example, individuals who learned at an early age to anesthetize their emotions with food may, as adults, have difficulty telling the difference between hunger and tiredness. Many who were sexually abused as children have fused together the emotions of fear and sexual arousal. As adults, they may feel "horny" when afraid, making them vulnerable to being victimized again. If force was used during their molestation, they may have fused together the emotions of rage and sexual arousal -- a setup for adult rapist behavior.

Those who were told "it's not nice to be angry" became disempowered in their ability to resolve injustices constructively. Those who were physically abused by parents have often fused together the emotions of love and hate. They love their parents, but hate what they did, and are unable to resolve the confusion. Therefore, they develop a different form of ambivalence (the fusion of love and hate). Leaving home, they relate to others through passive-aggressive, love-hate type of relationships.

126

Personal Application:
How can I sort all this out to find the cause and "cure" for my emotional woundedness?

Interpreting Our Emotional Life
Sorting this out requires that we learn how to get below our anger and fear and delve deep into the reservoir of inner pain associated with all of the past unresolved injustices in our life. Mankind's emotions are based -- not so much on what he/she experienced -- but rather, on their interpretation or understanding of those events, circumstances and situations. This interpretation and the resulting emotions are based on one's own unique sensory perceptions (or *phenomenological reality*), filtered through one's own unique belief system. It is from this -- one's personal interpretation -- that emotions spring forth.

Let me (Jim) illustrate this concept. In a college journalism course I participated in, the instructor repeatedly had a skit reenacted for his students. Typically, three students would unexpectedly enter the room and enact a mugging, then immediately leave the room. Each student in the class was then directed to write a short story reporting the event in as much detail as possible. As you can imagine, there were as many different stories as there were students in the classroom. No one was ever totally accurate. Moreover, there was *never* complete agreement over the number of persons involved the skit, which person or persons were perpetrators and which victims. The students were never agreement over other aspects, such as the clothes worn by the assailants, the weapons used, etc. Each student's perception was remarkably different.

Personal Application:
How can a person's perception and interpretation of an event vary so widely?

Whatever each individual experiences through his/her unique sensory perception is subsequently filtered through his/her individual belief systems. For example: If one student feared knives, he/she might recall the weapon as a knife while another, based on his/her past experience, might recall it being a pistol, or other weapon. Similarly, gender bias can affect the recall of the perpetrator's and/or victim's gender-identity.

Color and type of clothes will also affect one's perception. Imagine the differences in perception if one of the people in the skit wore a leather motorcycle jacket and one of the students was an avid motorcyclist while another had been beaten-up by a motorcycle gang! Grooming also plays a part in one's interpretation. Whether or not the men were clean-shaven or wore beards, whether or not the women appeared well dressed or unkempt, all call up to a person's consciousness past experiences. These experiences, when associated with our memories of those events, form beliefs -- beliefs as varied as human experience itself. Our emotions and our belief systems are, therefore, very individualistic.

To appreciate how differently people respond to a dramatic movie; the next time you watch one, take time to watch the people. Right in the middle of the most dramatic moments, some individuals may be crying, some cheering, others booing, and still others seem bored and uninterested. They are exhibiting very, very different emotions while watching the very same movie and apparently receiving the same visual sensory stimulation.

Or, picture yourself and one of your classmates or friends, walking through the woods hunting, looking for mushrooms or picking flowers. Imagine that you become separated and that you look up suddenly to see a large black bear. Now, imagine that your classmate or friend simultaneously, and unexpectedly, comes upon a very large black dog. Imagine that he/she believes it to be a bear. Suppose that both you and your classmate or friend, believe that bears are ferocious, deadly animals.

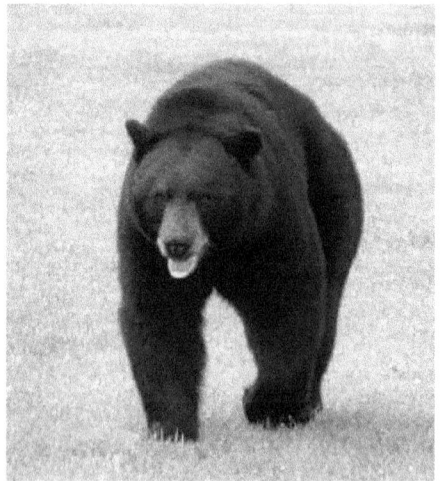

What emotion will each of you experience? _____

How much different will your emotions be? _____

In all likelihood, both of you will experience essentially the same emotion in the same intensity. In that instant, when both perceive that an animal is charging them, and both believe it is a bear, both will instantaneously react rather than stopping to analyze their sensory perceptions. Reactions come from one's belief systems stored deep within the subconscious mind. Since our subconscious mind literally knows no difference between fact and fiction (reality and fantasy), we will react out of fear, not fact.

Personal Application:
What does this have to do with anger-management?

Our reaction, in the case of a conflict, is the *automatic* triggering of our "fight or flight" response mechanism. It is the reaction one manifests when in the fight mode that we call anger. Anger then, is triggered: first by a loss, then by the resulting negative emotions felt as emotional pain, and finally by fear -- fear that the injustice will not be resolved, at least not without our personal intervention.

Personal Application:
How can I defuse, or desensitize, my fight-flight mechanism?

Unraveling, or more precisely, *defusing, or desensitizing,* this fight-flight triggering mechanism requires several steps:

- First, we must get below the anger, penetrate our fear, and get into our underlying emotions.

- Next, we must go even deeper, below our emotions, into the injustice itself.

- Finally, we must resolve -- or bring to closure -- these old injustices so that they no longer control us.

Getting below our anger requires great courage: courage to face our fear, and courage to temporarily re-experience the pain of past, unresolved injustices. Down below the anger are *real* emotions: feelings of being violated, controlled, ignored, embarrassed, demeaned, saddened, etc. These feelings are real and, they are important.

Personal Application:
Are my intimate relationships based on facts or emotions -- am I close to my partner because he/she agrees with me or, do I enjoy them because they provide positive emotional stimulation?

Human relationships, particularly intimate spousal and family relationships, are not based on facts. They are primarily based on emotions, or feelings.

Personal Application:
How do I really feel about my partner, child or other person I have been experiencing conflict with?

_____

Take a few minutes to get below any anger, bitterness and resentment you may feel. Pierce through your fear of losing that person, or being engulfed and controlled by them. How do you _feel_ about that person as a unique person (i.e., their character and physical traits? The two of you may be experiencing conflict, and perhaps have even endured episodes of abusive power and control. But, how do you _feel_ about them as a person?

Personal Application:
What are your relationship goals? _____

_____

Why did you and your partner get together initially?

_____

_____

What is it that you would _really_ like to accomplish in your relationship?

_____

_____

In all our years of counseling, we have yet to meet a single couple who got married to have someone to fight with. People normally marry for companionship, to enjoy intimacy, to share their lives, resources, and visions. Sadly, somewhere along our journey together, many of us forget our shared visions, goals and objectives. When we forget these things, we get off track and begin to experience conflict. When conflicts begin, barriers to desired intimacy spring up almost immediately. In response to these barriers, our anger (our intense motivation to break through the barrier and restore intimacy) can become aroused.

Personal Application;
Why does the desire for intimacy often result in family abuse or domestic violence?

_____

Frustrated over their inability to enjoy the intimacy expected, and lacking adequate communication and conflict-resolution skills, couples often resort to using the only relationship "skills" they know. They employ dirty-fighting techniques, abuse and violence. As a result, they get precisely what they do not want and most fear: rejection, further loss of intimacy, and strained -- if not broken -- relationships.

Personal Application;
How can I stop this destructive pattern?

_____

_____

One of the most successful methods of changing this self-defeating, destructive pattern is to begin to keep a journal of our anger episodes: what we felt, what we wanted, and what we did, and what the outcome was as compared with what we *really* wanted to accomplish.

Anger Log
On the following page is the format for employing this very important tool. With practice, one can use this tool to gain mastery over their anger.

Anger

Date & Time	Who was the Conflict with?	Where did the conflict occur?	Describe briefly what happened	Level of Anger On a scale Of 0 - 10

Log

What emotions were you feeling below your anger?	What did you do? (behavior, looks, words)	Did your Behavior Accomplish What you really wanted?	If not, what might you have done differently?

Assignment:
Your assignment, between now and your next lesson, is to maintain an accurate account, or log, of your anger. Each time you experience anger at any level of intensity, jot it down on your log. Then, when you have a few moments, complete the rest of the information for each incident. Note the time of day, where you were, what you were doing, who the conflict was with, what contributed to the conflict, and what occurred.

Then, rate the level of your anger on a scale of 0 to 10, with 0 being no discernible anger to 10 being intense, creating a compulsion to act on it.

Look below your anger. Discover what emotions you were feeling down below your anger. Refer to the previous emotional charts if necessary, to determine the location and severity of your emotions.

What did you do when you experienced the recorded incident? What did you say? What actions did you take, or refrain from taking?

Did your behavior (your words and actions) accomplish what you really wanted to accomplish to resolve the conflict you experienced? If not, what might you have done differently to achieve what you really wanted?

Don't neglect to complete this exercise. This assignment is essential to gaining an understanding of anger and how to appropriately manage it..

GLOSSARY

Elicit - to call forth or initiate

Severity - strength, intensity

Catatonic - a psychological state marked by profound stupor and immobility

Phenomena - (phenomenon) something that seems real to the senses, but cannot be observed objectively by others

KEY POINTS

- **Temperature Taking** - looking below our anger -- keeping in contact with our emotions and understanding them -- is the second primary emotion/anger-management tool.

- **The Acronym for fear:**

  - **F**alse
  - **E**vidence
  - **A**ppearing
  - **R**eal

- **Developmentally Arrested** - means that one's emotional age and development are dwarfed compared to their physical and intellectual development. **Also called the "adult-child" syndrome.**

- **Phenomenological Reality** - the perceived reality of an individual through the phenomena of his or her unique sensory perceptions.

Emotion = Energy-in-motion - a unique experience caused by a chemical change, or arousal, within our body.

CHAPTER 6
RELEASING NEGATIVE EMOTIONS

Review of Anger Logs
Review the anger log you kept as last lesson's assigned homework. If you failed to complete this assignment and you experienced any anger at all, please take time to do this assignment now. After keeping an anger log for several days, reflect on each incident listed. Compare your goals (e.g., what you *really* intended to accomplish in each incident) with how you acted (your behavior) and, look at what happened as a result (the outcome).

How well did your actions serve you in achieving your goal?

_____

If your actions did not support your efforts to attain your goal, how did you miss it?

_____

How far from your intended goal did your actions take you?

_____

Review objectively each incident you listed on your anger log. Now that the incident is past and, you are more calm, what might you have done differently, in each case, that would have more likely achieved your desired goal?

_____

Examining the Injustice
Focus on the incident you logged that created the most intense level of anger. Reflect on this incident for a few moments. Now, visualize yourself taking a time-out before you reacted to the emotional arousal. During this imaginary time-out, picture yourself standing at some distance and taking an emotional picture of the incident. Suppose that in this emotional snapshot you could visually see the activating event, the belief systems you relied on, your interpretation of the event, your reactive behavior, the other person's behavior and the ultimate outcome of the event.

Personal Application:
Was the level, or intensity, of your anger appropriate and relative?

_____

Was your anger really all about the present-moment incident, or were you reacting on past injustices as well as the present circumstance?

Was the behavior you acted-out directed toward the right person or object?

Did your behavior accomplish the goal of protecting and/or enhancing this relationship?

Or, did it perhaps get you what you feared most (i.e., rejection)?

If your anger was inappropriate, too intense, or misdirected, stop and ask yourself: *what*, at *what*, or with *whom* was I *really* angry?

Did the incident you logged remind you in any way of any earlier experiences in life that have never been resolved?

You may want to take a few minutes to ask yourself the following questions: does my partner's (or other person involved) anger, behavior, sound of their voice, etc., remind you of one of your parents, or another early-life authority figure with whom you experienced a lot of conflict?

If so, do you still feel anger or the underlying strong emotions when you recall your relationship with that person?

Is there a possibility that the recent incident you logged merely triggered some past baggage (old repressed memories) from your subconscious?

Is it possible that you are ambivalent: that you have fused together your love for the person and your displeasure of their behavior?

Ambivalence is a common form of emotional bondage that causes untold distress, resulting in the dysfunction and destruction of countless marriage partnerships.

Personal Application:
How can such emotional bondage effect my present relationships?

Men who, as boys, experienced a difficult, conflictual, controlling or enmeshed relationship with their mother; and women who, as girls, experienced similar relationship dynamics with their father, both tend to view those of the opposite sex through the "colored-glasses" of ambivalence.

As children, these girls and boys learned to hate their other-sex parent for their behavior, while continuing to love them as their parent who gave them life. As a result, they failed to realize the love and nurture they needed. They grew up believing that they must defend themselves from the opposite sex, while still clinging onto them for fear of loosing all love and nurture. As adults, these people tend to carry this belief, the underlying, unresolved negative emotions, and their reactive behavior into their marriage.

Personal Application:
What am I likely to experience in my adult relationships if I experienced ambivalence toward my same-sex parent?

When a person's ambivalence (the fusion of love and hate) is focused toward one's same-sex parent (father/son and mother/daughter) a somewhat different pattern emerges in adulthood. As these children grow up, they usually experience conflict and confusion in their relationships with authority figures: with teachers at school, Sunday school teachers, pastors, neighbors, employers, subordinates and even same-sex peers. While they may think their conflict is based on relationship difficulties with those they are currently interacting with, their conflicts are more often governed by past hurtful experiences that were never resolved.

Personal Application:
What if my childhood was great and my emotional wounds occurred later in life?

As we grow older, we experience numerous kinds of relationship pain: deaths in our family, divorce and/or separations, loss of jobs, etc. Each of these losses results in pain and fear: fear that our expectations in life will not be realized. Each loss triggers pain, pain triggers fear and fear triggers our motivation to correct the problem: experienced as anger. Each unresolved past incident has resulted in some level of suppressed or repressed anger. This anger, unless released, will eventually, be acted out -- either upon another person, or turned inward upon ourselves.

As incident after incident goes unresolved, and our compulsion to correct injustice goes unfulfilled, our inner stress becomes greater and greater, finally demanding release. Then -- often when we least expect it -- we lash out at someone, or something, only to realize later, that our actions were totally inappropriate, or way out of proportion to the event.

Appropriate conflict-management demands that one stay present-moment focused and centered on the situation or circumstance that is at hand. However, when the present moment incident reminds of past, unresolved incidents, staying present-moment focused is nearly impossible. The solution for this problem is to get in touch with past unresolved injustices, allow ourselves to temporarily feel the stress (our pent up negative emotions), and then release them. Employing this technique is a significant part of stress-management.

As a person's stress level climbs, his/her ability to manage stress simultaneously declines. This results in a significant portion of one's total emotional and intellectual energy being spent, or used up, suppressing or repressing these unresolved issues. Research estimates that the average, *emotionally healthy* person probably expends as much as *one-half* of their total psychological energy (subconscious thoughts and feelings) on this exhausting, totally nonproductive activity!

When you consider that the average, emotionally healthy individual. expends one-half of his/her psychological energy in this manner, imagine how much more energy an emotionally "dis-stressed" or "dis-eased," person expends. The emotional stress produced by this affects one's immune system, causes them to be more susceptible to disease, results in them developing auto immune diseases, such as arthritis and diabetes, and contributes to them suffering untold problems in their overall emotional health and well-being?

Personal Application:
What can one expect if they deplete their emotional reserves through unresolved issues?

As a person continues to use more and more of their psychological (emotional and intellectual) energy to keep old, unresolved issues buried, they have less energy to deal effectively with normal, everyday problems of life. Sooner or later they will come face to face with a present-moment crisis, such as an major illness, a major financial demand, finding out one of our children is in trouble, or experiencing a major disagreement with their partner. When this happens, they will discover that they have insufficient emotional reserves to manage the situation.

They have spent their emotional reserve "managing" their stress rather than resolving their issues. Now, unexpectedly, sometimes almost instantaneously, they discover that their psychological bank-account is overdrawn. They are emotionally bankrupt. When this emotional "bankruptcy" occurs, an individual begins to suffer the consequences. These consequences may vary from typical anxiety and depression manifestations to panic attacks, an episode of family violence, up to, and including, an emotional breakdown, heart attack, suicide or homicide. In other words, the consequences of pent-up stress can be life-threatening -- both to one personally, and devastating to their relationships.

The Cost of Stress

The following stress inventory, was adapted from the "Social Readjustment Rating Scale," by T.H. Holmes & R.H. Rame, Journal of Psychosomatic Research, 1967. The research it is based on, substantiates the negative impact stress has on one's health. This scale provides a fairly reliable projection of potential emotional and physical health problems, produced by high levels of stress. In addition to triggering numerous physical and psychological illnesses, stress is also a major factor in relationship conflict, abuse and violence.

Stress Management - Review the **STRESS SCALE** on the following page. Mark all of those events that you have experienced within the last two years. And, if an earlier event still arouses strong emotions within you whenever you think about them, mark those as well.

EVENT	# Times-	Imp.	Scor
Death of a spouse......................... ___		100	___
Divorce.................................... ___		73	___
Marital separation................... .... ___		65	___
Jail term.................................. ___		63	___
Death of a close family member.................. ___		63	___
Major personal injury or illness................... ___		53	___
Marriage.................................. ___		50	___
Fired from job.................. .... ___		47	___
Marital reconciliation.................... ___		45	___
Retirement................................ ___		45	___
Change in the health of a close family mbr.. ___		44	___
Pregnancy................................. ___		40	___
Sexual adjustment difficulty............... ...... ___		39	___
Increase in number of family members....... ___		39	___
Change in jobs or business adjustment....... ___		39	___
Change in financial state.................... ___		39	___
Death of a close friend............... .... ___		37	___
Change of profession, trade or vocation..... ___		36	___
Increase/decrease in arguments w/ spouse ___		35	___
Entering a mortgage of more than $50,000 ___		31	___
Foreclosure of a mortgage or loan.............. ___		30	___
Change in work responsibilities.................... ___		29	___
Son or daughter leaves home...................... ___		29	___
Trouble with your inlaws........................... ___		29	___
Outstanding personal achievement............. ___		28	___
Spouse begins or quits work......................... ___		26	___
Beginning or stopping school...................... ___		26	___
Change in living conditions.......................... ___		25	___
Change in personal habits........................... ___		24	___
Work related problems.......................... ___		23	___
Change in work hours or job conditions........ ___		20	___
Change in residence................................ ___		20	___
Change in school or educational program..... ___		20	___
Change in church activities.......................... ___		19	___
Change in recreation patterns...................... ___		19	___
Change in social activities.......................... ___		18	___
New mortgage or loan under $10,000.......... ___		17	___
Change in sleep habits........................... ___		16	___
Change in number of family get-togethers.... ___		15	___
Change in eating habits................................ ___		15	___
Vacation.. ___		13	___
Christmas holiday................................... ___		12	___
Minor violation of the law........................... ___		11	___
Totals		___	___

142

Directions for Scoring:

1) Compute your total stress level by multiplying the impact for each incident by the number of times you experienced that event or situation **during the past two years**, or longer if thinking about it still stirs your emotions.

2) Total your impact scores at the bottom to obtain your present stress level.
Record that score here: _____

3) Circle the scores for those things that **you** can never, never change (i.e., death, imprisonment, etc.),
Record that score here: _____

4) Subtract this score from your total impact score. The resulting score is the level of stress you would have if you just let go of those things you can never change.
Record the resulting score here: _____

5) Put a square around those things you cannot change now, due to a lack of time, resources or opportunity.
Record that score here: _____

6) Subtract this score from the resulting score under item 4.

Record the resulting score here: _____

The resulting number under item 6, is all the stress you would have deal with, if you let go of those things that you can never change, and set aside for the moment, those things that you do not presently have the ability to change.

Compare your total score with the following health-risk rating developed by Holmes and Rame:

- **0 - 149** = No significant emotional problem

- **150 - 199** = Mild life crisis (33% chance of illness within the next 12 months).

- **200 - 299** = Moderate crisis (50% chance of an illness within the next 12 months).

- **300 - +** = Major life crisis (80% + chance of illness or breakdown within the next year).

Stress and Your Health
Take another look at the total amount of your accumulated stress

(or distress), indicated by the inventory you just completed. Envision for a moment, that each point represents one pound. Imagine carrying around weight equaling the load of stress associated with all of the unresolved issues in your life. And, don't forget to include weight for other stress producing events experienced that are not on this list.

Personal Application:
How do you rate? Is your health and well-being at risk due the amount of stress in your life?

Now, take time to evaluate the various stressors in your life. Consider how many of these unresolved issues exist between you and your partner, between you and your children, between you and your parents, between you and your siblings, your neighbors, your employer, your employees, etc. How much are these unresolved issues affecting your health, well-being and enjoyment of life?

Stress: Distress or Eustress?
Stress comes in two varieties: distress and eustress. Both classes of stress are based on the same thing, *tension*. However, the two classes have significantly different outcomes. Distress causes physical illnesses, mental and emotional breakdowns, contributes to relational conflict, abuse, violence, separations and divorce. Eustress, like anger, is a motivation that when used correctly, produces change, releasing one's built-up tension. How one uses their stress, or tension, determines whether it matures into distress or eustress. And, this makes a great deal of difference in ones' overall health and well-being.

Personal Application:
What determines the difference between eustress and distress?

Eustress is stress that we become aware of before it becomes destructive, and utilize to effect positive change in our life. Constructive change results in the dissipation of our pent-up stress, or tension, and the restoration of a state of tranquility, serenity, or calmness. Distress, on the other hand, is by nature, destructive. It has to do with stress that we have stored up in our subconscious reservoir, and failed to release in a constructive manner. Stored-up, this type of stress (distress) causes disease and emotional disorders; and when at last let go of, is vented with such intensity, it contributes to abuse and violence.

Personal Application:
What can I do to reduce my stress or use it constructively?

_____

Avoiding the negative consequences of stress demands that we learn to reduce the level of our total stress, and properly manage stress which we cannot immediately release. The most effective approach to stress reduction is converting distress into eustress, then releasing this energy through constructive change.

Example:
To gain a clear understanding of the difference between distress and eustress, and their comparative impact on your life, imagine taking a rubber-band and stretching it between two pencils, as illustrated below.

If you keep on stretching and stretching the rubber band, what will happen? It will eventually break, of course. This is the effect of distress in our life. When we bottle up the stress produced by event after another, with no release, we will eventually reach the "breaking point."

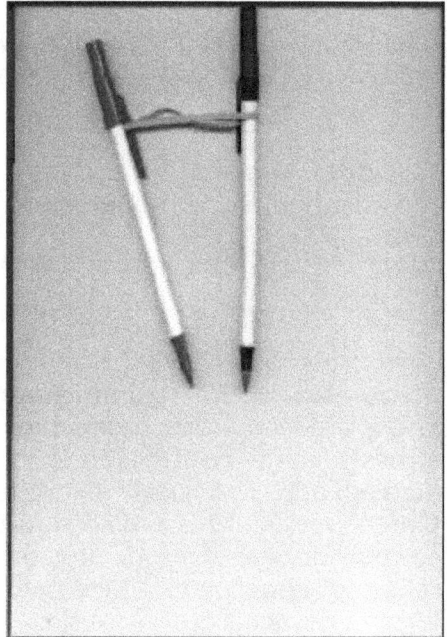

At the moment of release, our stress coping mechanisms (or abilities) and cognitive processes break down. Then, we react out of survival instinct. The reaction may be an emotional breakdown, physical illness or accident, or our acting out against another person in an episode of violence.

Imagine now that you become aware that this rubber band (your stress level) is approaching the limit of its elasticity. But, instead of continuing to stretch it until it breaks, you merely let go of one of the pencils before the band breaks. What happens? The pencil you let go of will probably go flying across the room. Simultaneously, the tension (or stress) in the rubber-band is dissipated and the rubber band (your stress level) returns to a slack (tranquil, calm or serene) condition.

This example illustrates what happens to one internally -- in their emotions. If we allow our stress to continue building unabated, at some point we experience an emotional breakdown. Stress (or tension) is but a message, crying aloud, **"Let go**!**,**" **"Let go**!**"** Letting go of the injustice that produced the stress, the individual or individuals we hold responsible for the injustice, and the resulting electrochemical charge (our resulting emotions), will release our pent-up stress. This allows us to avert danger and return to a state of serenity, or calm tranquility.

Stress-management vs. Stress-reduction
Personal Application:
What is the difference between stress-reduction and stress-management?

The act of letting go (or releasing our tension), is called "stress-reduction." Learning to avoid stress-producing situations and/or to release unavoidable negative events quickly, rather than allowing them to build up and cause problems, is called "stress-management."

Personal Application:
What techniques can one use to reduce their stress level?

Stress-Reduction Techniques
There are numerous techniques employed in stress-reduction and stress-management. Some of the more prominent include: biofeedback, physical exercise, drugs and guided imagery. Biofeedback utilizes a discomforting, mild electric shock, applied to discourage stress producing thought processes. Physical exercise releases endorphins (stress-releasing chemicals) in the brain. Pharmaceuticals (prescription drugs) attempt to stimulate the release of endorphins or block the reuptake of various reward hormones. Various types of guided imagery, or visualization techniques, can be used to help one release stress.

Personal Application:
Take another look at the stress inventory you completed. Reflect on the differences between your present level of stress; what your stress level would be if you rid yourself of the stress associated with those things that you can never, never change); and then rid yourself of those things you cannot resolve at the moment.

These differences represent how much your overall health and well-being will improve, if you merely lay down (or release) all of the stressors in the last two categories.

How much better would you feel right now, if you released all of that stress -- putting it out of your mind and off your "worry list."?

Imagine how much your health-risk factor would diminish if you let these stressor go, and the few, remaining stressors, was the only emotional tension in your life.

Great News!
This stress is the *only* stress that you have to continue to deal with. Moreover, it is the only stress you have the ability to resolve at this moment in time. The stress you have been carrying around, damaging your health and negatively affecting your relationships, can be significantly reduced by letting go of those things that you can never, never change; and properly managing those things that you cannot change at the present moment, treating them in a completely different manner from worrying about them.

Letting go
Personal Application:
If you are like the "average" person, you have been expending more than one-half of your total, finitely limited, psychological energy trying to change things you can never, never change and worrying about those things you simply do not have the ability to change at the present moment.

Trying to do what you simply cannot do depletes your physical, emotional, intellectual and spiritual energies. It is tiring, and discouraging. No matter how hard you try, you can not do, what you can not do.

Personal Application:
What is the effect of trying to resolve these issues with your present resources, limitations and energy?

Trying to do what can't be done eventually makes a person just want to give up. The resulting sense of hopelessness also encourages many to go out and drink, use drugs, gamble, or get involved in most anything that will temporally anesthetize their thoughts, emotions and memories. In this state, we don't have to face our inability to resolve these issues, or admit that we are powerless. However, they are still, very much, alive.

The outcome of pent-up stress is that it consumes us. It keeps us problem-focused rather than goal-oriented and solution-focused. Unless we figure out how to resolve those items we enclosed in circles and squares, we simply cannot stay present-moment focused. And, unless we become present-moment focused we cannot recapture enough of our emotional energy to effectively work on those lesser issues -- the few remaining ones.

More critical than any of these concerns is that fact that unless we can figure out how to reduce our stress, we may become another statistic. Unable, or unwilling, to release our stress, we will remain at risk for suffering from one or more psychosomatic illnesses, (i.e., falling victim to some accident, suffering a relapse into alcohol or drug abuse, picking up some other obsessive/compulsive behavior, experiencing recurrent conflict and potential for episodes of violence, perhaps even having a heart attack or stroke).

Personal Application:
Is it really possible to be free from the load of stress I carry?

There is a method, readily available, that anyone can use to free themselves from most of the unnecessary stress (or "baggage") they carry around. This method doesn't involve the use/abuse of alcohol, prescription or illicit drugs, any other mood-altering substance or experience. Nor, does it normally require expensive biofeedback treatments. The method we recommend is a process available to everyone, everywhere -- and it's free!

In the next lesson you will find out how to use this method to release (literally let go of) all those stressors you circled and drew squares around. Better yet, you will discover how to release all of this stress -- some of which you may have been carrying around for years -- in just one sitting! You will also learn how to effectively manage the small level of residual stress. Finally, you will learn how to keep your present stress level low and manageable.

Homework
Take time between now and your next lesson to review your stress test. Add to it any other unresolved life stressors you have experienced that are included on the list. *Be sure to save your*

stress test scores so that you can refer to them during the next lesson.

GLOSSARY

Ambivalence - the fusion of opposing emotions (i.e., love and hate) causing us to become emotionally frozen -- incapable of experiencing one emotion without sensing the other.

Subconscious - a thought process lying below our conscious focus, generally believed to be our right-brain, involving our affective (e.g., emotional) thought processes.

Visualize - imagine, picture, experience emotionally.

KEY POINTS

- **Two types of stress and the meaning of each**
  - distress
  - eustress

- **Stress-reduction Technique**s:
  - biofeedback
  - exercise
  - drugs
  - visual imagery

CHAPTER 7
RECONCILING PAST INJUSTICES

Review:
In the last lesson, we discussed some of the effects that stress has on our being: body, soul (mind) and spirit. We learned that stress, when pent-up, can result in diminished health, even wielding life-threatening consequences. In this lesson, we will begin the work of reducing our stress level, while simultaneously improving our functionality.

First, take a few moments to review the results of your stress test. Look once again at your total score and how it was broken down between your total stress; that associated with those things you can never change; that associated with those things you may be able to resolve someday, but not at the present; and the remaining stress, if the other was released or set aside.

Personal Exercise: Releasing Stress Through Visualization
Focus, for a few moments, on those events that you circled -- those things you cannot change. By your own admission, you acknowledged that you can never, never, never change these things. Holding onto and investing *any* emotional energy into things you can never, never, never change is fruitless. It will, in time, result in your emotional bankruptcy, manifest through a physical, mental or emotional breakdown.

Holding onto those old injustices -- those past experiences that wounded us so much we want to avoid even thinking about them -- actually control us, because we are using a great deal of our energy hanging on to them. We often hear statements from students like: "So and so did such and such to me, and I will never forget it," "I will never let it go of it," "I will never forgive them."

When we make statements like this, we *think* that **we** are in control. The truth is, we have given the very person we hold responsible, and the unforgiven event that wounded us, control over our life. They have our very life in their hands, and they are relentlessly draining away our very life-force.

Personal Application:

Reflect for a few minutes on the unresolved issues in your life. Who, through unforgiveness, have you become attachment to, giving them permission to control your life?

_____

How can you stop this control?

_____

_____

The best resolution, or method of release, is to "let go" of (or release) these past injustices, the perpetrator and our associated memories, to God as you know Him -- a process called *forgiveness*.

Let's demonstrate how you can effortlessly let go, using your own creativity.

To accomplish this, you need to stop trying to keep all of those old hurts and wounds buried. This merely misleads one into believing that they have them "under "control." Allowing them to surface, is the first step in letting go of them. To experience this, find a comfortable chair, sit back, relax. In a few minutes you can actually experience significant stress reduction through this visualization exercise.

Note: It may help if you play some soft background music while you follow the instructions that follow. Pause for a few seconds between each statement or phrase. To get the most from this exercise, you may want to record the following meditation, pausing between each statement, then play it back to yourself while you are in a quiet meditative state):

· Sit back in your chair, get comfortable and relax. . . .

· Put your feet flat on the floor a little bit out in front of your knees. . . .

· Open your hands, relax them, resting them on your thighs . . .

- Imagine you are holding a Raggedy-Ann doll. . . .

- See how limp she is? . . .

- Imagine that you are just as limp as she . . .

- Imagine that she is slowly rocking back and forth . . .

- Imagine you can see yourself -- your face -- in her face. . . .

- Begin to gently rock back and forth like Raggedy-Ann is . . .

- Close your eyes, letting your head fall forward onto your chest
. . .

- Open your mouth by just letting your chin relax and fall. . . .

- Take a deep breath - breathe in . . .

- hold it a few seconds and feel the oxygen rush. . . .

- Now relax - letting your breath go . . .

- Push the last of the air out from your lungs. . . .

- Take another deep breath . . . breathe in . . . hold it . . . feel
the oxygen rush. . . .

- Relax . . . let your breath go and push it from your lungs. . . .

- Continue taking deep breaths, holding them until you feel the
oxygen rush, then relaxing and letting your breath go. . . .

- With each breath you take, relax deeper and deeper (taking
about ten to twelve deep breaths). . . .

- Now, let's imagine re-experiencing an early-life injustice . . .

- Imagine that the room you are sitting in morphs into a time
tunnel, and your chair becomes a special time-travel capsule .

- Imagine yourself traveling backwards - backwards in time. .

- Travel back . . . back . . . back in time . . . Back to your
childhood. . .

- Imagine traveling back to, and seeing once again, the earliest home you can remember living in, or perhaps the earliest home you felt violated or abused in. . . .

- Find the child you were then, perhaps playing in the yard . . .
- Approach and introduce yourself to the child you were then. . .

- Tell your inner-child that you are his/her future and you have come back to get acquainted . . .

- Get down on your knees and play with your little inner-child for a few moments . . .

- Now, take your child's hand and ask him/her to take you into the house where you lived so long ago . . .

- Walk into the home -- hand in hand -- and see yourself there at the age you were way back then . . .

- Now, for a brief time, become that little child again, and begin to walk through the house. . . .

- Wander slowly through each room . . .

- Take time to look at the colors of the paint or wallpaper on the walls, look at the carpets or linoleum on the floor . . .

- Look at the pictures on the walls, and the furniture that is in each room. . . .

- Go from room to room, especially visiting the room where you slept . . .

- Now visit the places where you played, those places you feared, and your parents room. . .

- Stop and listen to the sounds going on in the house . . .

- Take time to smell the odors in the house -- odors of cooking, canning, etc. . . .

- Feel the emotions in the house, the stress and tension between your parents or others, feel the anxiety, sadness, depression, and any anger you were subjected to. . . .

- Re-experience the emotions you experienced back then as you remember your relationship with your mother . . .
- Now think about your father and feel the emotions his memory evokes . . .

- Think about anyone else living in your childhood home . . .

- Find your parents, or other primary caretakers. Walk to the front room and stand before them.

- Now, step out and become your adult self again and pick up your inner child (your little boy or girl) . . .

- Whisper in your inner-child's ear, telling him/her that you are his/her future and you've returned to get him . . .

- Assure him/her you want to take him/her with you, to protect them and help them become everything God designed them to be . . .

- Look at your parents and/or other primary caretakers and tell them: "I am _____'s (insert your name) future. I have come to take him/her home with me. . .

- It is time for me to help him/her grow up and become all that God intended him/her to be . . .

- Thank your parents or caretakers for what they provided for you and forgive them for not providing, or not being able to provide, what you *really* needed . . .

- Holding your little "inner-child" in your arms, go to the door, then turn and tell your parents, or caretakers, good-bye. . . .

- Open the door, take a deep breath, step outside, turn and wave good-bye one more time, then close the door and walk to the road or street your childhood home faced . . . .

- Turn, and walk up the road. Every time you look back over your shoulder, the house will get smaller and smaller. . . .

- Pretty soon, you will come to a corner or curve in the road. As you go around that curve or corner, you won't be able to look back anymore. . . .

- Around the corner you will meet other people -- people from your present and perhaps your future -- people you can trust to help you raise your inner-child to become all that God intended him/her to be. . . .

- Introduce your inner-child to each of these people, asking them to help you grow up and become all that you can be. . . .

- After introducing your little inner-child to each of these people, take him/her home with you. . . .

  Find a comfortable chair or couch . . . sit down and hold your little inner-child on your lap. . . .

- Hold him/her close to you, putting your arms around him/her, sharing your innermost love and receiving theirs . . .

- Promise your little child that you will never, never leave, abandon or reject him/her . . .

- That you will never abuse him/her . . .

- That you will always listen to him/her . .

- That you will always do your best to meet his/her needs and fulfill his/her desires. . .

- Promise to always be there for him/her, promise to always protect him/her from harm. . . .

- Love your little inner-child again, telling him/her how glad you are that they came home with you . . .

- Now, imagine that they are getting sleepy and you put him/her down for a nap. . . .

- Now, go back to your couch or chair and sit down . . .

- As you sit down, imagine you find yourself sitting in "Daddy God's" ("Abba Father's") lap . . .

- Hear Daddy God telling you, "I will never, never abandon or reject you . . .

- I will never abuse you . . .

- I will always listen to you . . .

- I will meet your needs and fulfill your positive desires". . . .

- As you sit in the safety of God's lap, hear Him remind you that He came to take your pain and give you the oil of gladdens . .

- Reconnect emotionally with all the pain you felt as you visited your old childhood home, and became reacquainted with your inner-child . . .

- Cup your hands in out in front of you, then in mind's eye (your imagination), place all your pain and fear in your cupped hands, along with all the injustices you experienced, and the person/s who inflicted that pain . . .

- Begin letting your negative emotions, the painful experiences and those who were responsible go by releasing them from your solar-plexus and inner-being (gut feeling) . . .

- Let the pain flow up toward your shoulders . . . into your arms . . . out through your arms . . . into your cupped hands . . .

- As you begin to feel the release, you may wish to revisit -- in your imagination -- other painful situations in your life -- those that you can never, never change, and let go of them. . .

- Do the same with each of those injustices -- focus each injustice, the pain, and the person/s involved in inflicting the pain outside of you -- into the palms of your hands. . . .

- Now, envision God, or Christ, as you know Him coming up to you . . . Him looking at you lovingly, inviting you to give all your burdens to Him. . . .

- Reach your cupped hands out toward Him and release all of those injustices, all of those people who wounded you, and all of your emotional pain . . . releasing them to Him. . . .

- After you have released it all to God, receive back from Him the oil of joy -- his love, joy, comfort and healing. . . .

- Imagine your cupped hands overflowing with His love, joy, peace, comfort and healing . . .

- Draw your hands toward your chest, allowing these positive emotions to pass into your inner-being . . .

- Absorb them, feeling the pleasant, warm sensations flow through your entire being . . .

- After you have absorbed His love, joy, comfort and healing, sit back for few moments to just bask in perfect peace and serenity . . .

- As you have taken this time-travel trip, you have experienced the powerful process, of *letting go -- letting go* and giving it all to God . . .

- This letting go -- this release -- is the process that we are so often so fearful of -- it is that process called *forgiveness!* . . .

- Forgiven, neither the people who perpetrated injustices against you, the injustices themselves, nor the pain, can ever again control your life -- they are gone . . .

Exercise Two
Try to flow from exercise one into exercise two as smoothly as possible -- if possible, without taking a break. It will be much easier to do so if you have previously recorded the first exercise and play it back while you just enjoy the experience.

- Now that you have released all of that stress you've stored up about things that you can never, never change, take a few moments to feel the difference . . .

- Sense the emotional release as you let go of these events; feel the difference in your energy level -- your spiritual, psychological and physical strength. . . .

- With your eyes still shut, imagine taking all of those events that you do not have the resources and/or ability to change today, and see yourself writing each issue or injustice down on a slip of paper . . .

- Now, see yourself placing all of those slips of paper into a fruit jar . . .

- Imagine that you are canning them, and placing them in your freezer, your pantry, or on your closet shelf . . .

- They will be safe there, and since you don't have the immediate ability or resources to change these things, choose to leave them there, until you have the necessary resources and ability to resolve them, one by one . . .

- As you gain the ability and/or resources to deal with these preserved issues, you can retrieve the jar and remove the slip of paper containing the issue you are now prepared to, and capable of, resolving . . .

- Investing emotional energy in an attempt to resolve these issues, prior to accumulating adequate resources and abilities, will only result in emotional fatigue and/or breakdown . . .

- Take time now to enjoy how much lighter you feel with the un-resolvable issues gone and the issues you can't resolve now safely stored away until the time comes when you can deal with them . . .

- Feel your renewed energy, and the new empowerment you have to work on those few remaining issues . . .

- Begin now to slowly become more aware of, feeling, the chair you are sitting on . . .

- Now, feel the floor beneath your feet again . . .

- Become more aware of everything around you, becoming just a bit restless . . .

- Take a couple of deep breaths and open your eyes slowly, feeling calm, relaxed and full of renewed energy -- like you have had a good long nap . . .

Letting Go & Forgiveness
As you completed the visualization process of letting go of the past injustices, the person or persons who hurt you, and your emotions attached to those injustices, you have experienced the powerful process of letting-go, called *forgiveness*.

Why has forgiveness always been so difficult for me? _____

Regardless what one has been told in the past, one cannot release past injustices by making an intellectual decision to forgive. The reason that this is so ineffective, is that the pain we experienced during past injustices was emotional, and perhaps spiritual, not intellectual. You cannot intellectually let go of emotional and spiritual pain.

Asking someone to let go, to intellectually forgive, their emotional and spiritual wounds is much like someone asking you to let go of their glasses while seated across the room from you, holding them firmly in their hand.

You cannot let go of their glasses unless and until you first take hold of them. You can only let go of, what you hold, or have a hold on. Therefore, in order to let go of past injustices and the associated emotional pain, you must allow yourself to take hold of them -- to re-experience those incidents as clearly as possible in as much detail as possible, your imagination. Then, and only then, can you choose to let go of the pain, not from your intellect, but from your emotional center. You can only let go of the pain while you are experiencing it, just as you did in the foregoing guided visualization exercise.

To clarify the picture of the past event or events you wish to release, take time to get in touch with your sensory information about those events. Recall what kind of a day it was when the event occurred. Was is sunny, cloudy, perhaps rainy or snowy? Picture once again what you saw. Listen once again to the sounds you heard. Notice once again any odor or fragrance that filled the air. Do you remember touching anything? If so, feel yourself touching it again. Were you eating anything? If so, remember its taste, letting your taste buds replicate that taste. Remember the emotions you experienced? Allow yourself to sense them once again.

Now, being once again in touch with your sensory information about the event, consider your feelings. Are they appropriate in focus and intensity to the event? If not, there may be other past events you need to revisit and release. If your emotions seem more intense than justified, you may have experienced other, similar but more hurtful experiences. If, on the other hand, your emotional response seems insufficient, this might indicate you were desensitized to this form of injustice over time. An example of this occurs when a child is groomed by a sexual predator, prior to the actual sexual abuse.

Personal Application:
What's the purpose behind this visualization process?

_____

As you traveled along, on our little imaginary trip in exercise one, you actually converted a great deal of *distress* into *eustress.* How? Our subconscious mind thinks in pictures and symbols. Therefore, when you imagined letting go of the old injustices you were anchored to, your subconscious mind accepted your release as real. As you gave them to God, your subconscious mind accepts this, and when you received God's oil of gladness in exchange, your subconscious mind embraced the fact that you are loved by Father God.

This exercise allowed your pent-up stress, once released, to change the way you look at those old issues, and feel about the people involved. This exemplifies what King Solomon penned so long ago: "As a man thinks in his heart, so it will be" (Pr 23:7). As old injustices are released, it will enable you to look forward rather than back, establishing and moving toward new goals that will result in new behaviors, attitudes and beliefs.

Personal Application:
How does visualization relate to forgiveness?

_____

_____

This process of 'release' (or letting-go), properly understood, *is* a process called *forgiveness.* Forgiveness is not an instantaneous act or momentary event. It is actually much more of a process -- a process that is often grossly misunderstood.

Personal Application:
What then, is the real meaning of forgiveness?

_____

_____

To adequately answer this, we need to look at some of the things that forgiveness is not. For instance, forgiving injustices does *not* mean:

- "Forgive and forget" - The human mind is not designed to forget -- that characteristic is divine!

- "It was all right" - It certainly wasn't all right for anyone to act unjustly against you.

- "It never happened" - The injustice *did* happen, or at least you believe it did, and you were hurt by the injustice -- real or imagined.

- "It was all my fault anyway" - Being hurt emotionally is rarely one's own fault.

- "We won't ever talk about it again" - You may need to talk about it many times before you realize complete resolution . . . before it loses its control over you and the energy dissipates.

Forgiveness has come into the English language from an old Latin word that literally means "To give as before" (i.e., to relate to the offending person in the same manner you did before the offense occurred). This is probably better understood by looking at the root words the Latin word adopted into English was derived from. They both come from ancient languages and are found frequently in the Bible. One of these words is from the Old Testament, the other from the New Testament.

In the New Testament, the Greek word that translated *forgive* in English is "affirm" (or "aphiemi") which means to let go (release, yield up, or send away). In the Old Testament, the Hebrew words most commonly translated *forgive* are "Calach," which means to pardon, and "Nacah," which means to absolve (release and yield up). Contextually, these words are often found in conjunction with other Hebrew words such as "Caphar," which means to declare or speak out, and "Cashab," which is translated "to reckon," an old accounting term from which we get the English words, reconcile and reconciliation (referring to the balancing of accounts).

Personal Application:
What can we learn about forgiveness from the meaning of these words?

_____

When we would take time to reflect on the meaning of these words, and the context they are used in, we discover the following basic principles:

Aphiemi refers to the letting go, yielding up, or releasing of a trapped animal -- in this case, letting go of the individual whom we hold responsible for any past injustice.

This involves releasing our emotional pain, the person or persons who inflicted the injustice upon us, and the events themselves. (In secular usage of ancient times, these words were often used within the context of releasing an animal from a snare or trap).

- *Calach* refers to the absolving (or pardoning) of the offender. This infers a legal, or court action.

- The declaration that the account (injustice) was now reconciled (balanced the accounts),

- The last aspect of the absolution involved the public declaration of the offender's pardon.

Who's Work is What?
The problem we have in carrying out the process of forgiveness usually reposes in the fact that we are trying to do God's part and expecting Him to do ours.

Our task is first and foremost to let go -- to release and yield up to God, the offense, the offender and our wounded emotions. God's part lies in balancing, or reconciling the accounts; and, in a joint act with us, the absolution or pardon of the perpetrator.

Finally, there is another part to be performed by us. It involves our speaking out (or declaring) the offender's pardon.

We cannot do God's part because our understanding of reconciling injustices lies primarily in the concept of punishment. We want to go after the guilty person with vengeance -- to get even, hurt and perhaps even destroy the offender. Contrast this with God's declaration that vengeance belongs to Him, and the fact that His method of reconciliation is very different from our own. We go after people to hurt them and get even. He goes after people --

sometimes *with* a vengeance -- to bring them to repentance, change them and save them.

In truth, if we allow ourselves to get below the level of our anger into our *real* emotions, then release our pain, mankind's basic, underlying desire is, in most cases, to effect change. Unfortunately, however, we do not have the knowledge nor the ability to change another person. When we try, we attempt to accomplish the task through force.

When we attempt to change another person using force, power and control, all we really do is engage their defense mechanisms, their resistance, their obstinence and defiance. We then become engaged in a power struggle not too dissimilar from that pictured between the two sumo wrestlers depicted right.

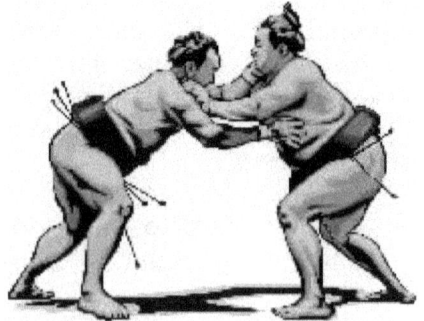

In reality, the other's obstinance and defiance is rarely against change. It is, rather, an attempt by that other person to protect their own identity -- to keep us from making them into our "clone."

Personal Application:
If I cannot change my partner, what hope is there for our relationship?

_____

_____

While we cannot change another person, there is one thing that any of us can readily change. We can always change ourselves. Even that is, sometimes, a major task. When it comes to the change we would like to see in our partner or other person, the best way to realize this is to take our hands off of them, quit trying to control them verbally and emotionally, and let go of them. We need to let go, and allow God be God in their lives. When *God* begins to change a person's life, then, and *only* then will the account between them and ourselves becomes reconciled, or balanced.

Let me illustrate this principle. If you have ever been in business, or conducted business with acquaintances, you have probably experienced, at some time or another, a person taking advantage of you. You may have experienced someone who owes you money, who continues to ignore their responsibility. Worse yet, they may even deny they owe you.

There are several alternatives you might employ in such circumstance, in an attempt to "balance your accounts." First, you could try to "hurt the hurter" (go after them and inflict physical injury or emotional pain, just to get even).

Personal Application:
Perhaps you have even tried this. How well does this it work?

_____

_____

This method might gain you a bit of personal satisfaction; however, it might also create barriers between you and other members of your and/or their family. It might also result in your arrest, conviction and possibly even some time in jail. At the best, it will inflict greater damage to your relationship with that person, and with those who love them.

A second alternative you might try, would be to ignore the debt -- to just forget about it. Most of us have attempted this at least once or twice and know that it does nothing to solve the problem. When we try to ignore an unresolved matter, it seems that we are continually reminded of the injustice and every time we think about it, we re-experience the pain, thus reinforcing our sense of injustice: the loss, pain, fear and anger.

Every time we see a person whom we have an unsettled account with, we remember the injustice. When we see or hear about another person being treated in a similar fashion, we tend to think about our own situation, once again re-experiencing the injustice and loss. We may see the offender on the street and turn away from him/her, perhaps even crossing the street to get away from them. Even that doesn't work, we still re-experience the injustice, recall the loss and pain, and sense our anger.

Personal Application:
If these methods don't work is there any technique that does?

_____

A third, much more successful method of resolving the injustice, or balancing the account, has to do with combining, or blending, the meanings of the Greek and Hebrew words relating to the individual aspects of 'forgiveness'. Collectively, they have quite appropriately been translated into English as "*forgive*" -- giving to the other person as we did before the injustice. This involves an understanding of just whose responsibility it is to do what; and what we are responsible to give one who has committed an injustice against us.

Settling Our Accounts:
Contemplating on the settlement of accounts, and using financial management as a metaphor, consider the following alternative: Instead of taking things into your own hands and trying to get even, or trying to ignore the problem and the guilty party, you could retain a collection agency to represent your interests. I have had to personally use that approach on occasion, and when I do, the effect is very different than when I undertake the task of collection on my own. Under the best arrangement the debt is assigned to *them* -- the collection agency. It is no longer *my* debt to collect, but theirs.

They have methods and means at their disposal that I lack in order to collect debts. For example, they can report the person's financial irresponsibility internationally, effectively stopping them from buying on credit. They can spend a great deal more time and effort on the matter than I, frequently reminding the person of their obligation and the consequences of ignoring it. If it becomes necessary, they can even take that person to court, garnish their wages, attach their property, etc.

Another distinct advantage to my assigning past due debts to a collection agency is that due to their expertise, the probability of them collecting the debt is much greater than mine. Thus, I stand a good chance to recover at least a portion of the debt once they collect it. The principle benefit, however, is that having made such an assignment, I can face that person without experiencing negative emotions. I have confidence -- in light of my established relationship with the collection agency -- that my debtor will eventually have to change his/her behavior. Moreover, if I am more careful in my dealings with that individual, I can still do business with them in the future -- giving to them as I did before the injustice occurred.

Managing Everyday Stress:
Your emotional health can be dramatically improved by forgiving (or letting go) of the un-resolvable, and canning (or storing away) those things that cannot be resolved at present. After completing these tasks, you can now concentrate your focus on those events that you have the time, the talent and the resources to resolve. After all, these are the only stressors that you have the ability and

resources to solve today. Recognizing this, why focus on, or expend your time, talents or resources on any of the others?

Expending your finite, limited, emotional energy on issues you can never, never change; or on those that you have neither the resources nor ability to change today, would be comparable to flushing your limited supply of money down the toilet! When one is bankrupt -- financially or emotionally -- they cannot take care of their present needs.

Now that you have trimmed your list of stressors down to those you have the ability and resources to change now, review them carefully. Take time to prioritize them from the most difficult problem, requiring the greatest effort and resources to solve, down to the one that easiest to resolve. Now, imagine taking your priority list and turning it upside down so that the more easily resolved problems are at the top; with the resolution problems becoming more difficult as you proceed down the list.

After you have arranged your list in this manner, focus your problem resolution efforts on your easiest problem, rectifying that issue before you move on to the next. By proceeding in this fashion, each issue settled will empower you. Each problem resolved will restore lost physical and emotional energy. This will give you increasingly greater abilities to undertake work on the next issue, then the next one, and so on, until you have resolved all the problems on your list.

To many this seems backward. Some believe that to relieve the most stress, it would be best to take care of the largest, the most pressing problem first. However, this is not the case. To understand this better, imagine that you owe eleven creditors a total of twenty thousand dollars ($20,000). One you owe ten thousand dollars ($10,000), and you owe the other ten one thousand ($1,000) each. Envision how you would feel if all of eleven of your creditors were hounding you for money. Imagine that each creditor has calling, sending certified letters and pressuring you for payment in full, in every way possible, for several months.

Suppose that you have been making small payments to each, only to see the principle amounts grow due to penalties and interest.

Imagine that you have now exhausted your bank account, and can make no payment at all. Assume that these creditors have no concern for your plight. They continue their collection activities, creating a tremendous amount of stress in your life. Visualize how you would feel when you have reached the point where you have no resources, and begin to believe there is no way out. You might quickly lose hope and begin to feel helpless. You see financial ruin, bankruptcy or death, as your only alternatives.

Personal Application:

Now, imagine that feeling this way, you pick up your mail and with unbelievable glee, discover you have won a $10,000 lottery or sweepstakes. You suddenly feel like you have just discovered the pot of gold at the end of a rainbow! What will you do with the money? Go on a spending spree to release the stress you've been feeling, hoping you will find another $10,000 from another source in the near future? Or, would you pay your bills?

If you decide to do the prudent thing and pay your bills, which one will you pay first? Will you pay the one creditor you owe $10,000 to get him off your back? Will you proportion it out, paying each creditor half of what you owe them, hoping to make them all a little bit happier and buy more time? Or, will you pay a bit on each and take a vacation with the rest, to reduce your stress level?

Entertain, for a moment, the effect of each alternative:

1) A spending spree may temporarily relieve the pressure you've been under, but will do nothing to resolve your problems.

2) Paying the creditor you owe $10,000 may get rid of your "biggest" problem, but it will still leave you with ten creditors to hound you and add more stress to your life.

3) Paying them all half, and hoping to buy more time, which at first blush sounds attractive, will leave you still owing all eleven creditors. Based on your past experience, they will, no doubt, all continue to press you for payment in full.

4) Paying them all something and taking a vacation to relieve your stress no doubt sounds tempting, but this would probably anger all of your creditors, making them increase their collection activity against you.

Personal Application:
What then is the best solution, and why?

_____

_____

The best solution would be to pay off the ten creditors you owe $1,000 each. If you choose this scenario, you will have freed yourself completely from ten (91%) of your creditors. This will leave you only one to pay. And, by paying off the other nine, you will have greatly improved your ability to make regular payments on this one remaining account.

Personal Application
Life is full of stressful situations. How can I best manage the ongoing stress in my life?

_____

_____

Stress Management Techniques
Take a few minutes to review your list of remaining stressors. As you do, note that every item you marked necessitates a change of one sort or another to bring resolution.

While change releases stress, all change, good or bad, also produces stress. Recognizing this fact, determine that you will not make changes in your life, just for the sake of change. Remember that each change -- however good in the long run -- will temporarily deplete your emotional energy reserve.

Learn to manage the stress in your life by learning to manage changes. As you do, you will begin to recover your physical, mental, emotional and spiritual energies. Your overall happiness and enjoyment of life will increase. This and several other stress-management techniques we will introduce, are readily available and easy to use.

Personal Application
Identify those stress-management skills you are familiar with?

_____

Some of the less common, most effective stress-management skills include the following:

- Address your easiest problem, solving it first, then address the next one, working your way toward the most difficult.

- Don't cluster changes. Remember that every change produces stress temporarily.

- You may need to make a number of changes in your life, but in so far as possible, make only one change at a time, allowing your life to adjust before making another change.

- Don't ignore life's problems. This allows problems to grow until they gain control over you, instead of you controlling them.

- Remember, one of the major stressors in life, is the lack of control.

- Don't intentionally put yourself in situations, circumstances, or engage in events that are, by nature, out of control.

A person's stress is not proportionate to the difficulty of a task. Its intensity is determined by whether or not one can control the activity and the outcome of that task.

For example, consider the probable stress level experienced by workers in various vocations. Imagine that in group "A", one person works as a waitress, another as an elevator operator, and another as a taxicab driver. In group "B", one person is brain surgeon, another a certified public accountant, and another a commercial pilot.

Which group of professionals, or tradesmen do you think will experience the most stress, and which group the least, amount of stress; and why?

Most_____

Least_____

At first glance, one might think that the more complicated professions, involving detailed tasks, such the as commercial pilot, accountant and brain surgeon would be the most stressful. Quite the contrary. Even though their vocations require painstaking accuracy, the brain surgeon, the accountant and the pilot all have the ability to exercise a high degree of control over their work schedules and duties.

In contrast, the waitress, the elevator operator and the taxi driver are essentially on-call: controlled by the needs and desires of those they serve. Their schedules and the particular duties they must fulfill to satisfy their customers are comparatively, largely outside of their control. The ability to control one's own destiny is much less stressful than being controlled by others.

Stress & Anger-management
Practicing stress-reduction and stress-management skills will goes long way in helping an individual reduce the level of their anger, and manage it more effectively. A major contributing factor in the relationship between stress-management and anger-management, involves biochemical reactions. When one is stressed, they produce high levels of the hormones, cortisol and norepinepherine, the body's endogenous adrenaline. These hormones are designed to prepare one for the fight and flight response. This is accomplished in part, by these hormones inhibiting the production of other hormones such as Dopamine, GABA and Serotonin.

Dopamine has been called, 'the pleasure hormone,' in that it increases the level of pleasure, joy and happiness one experiences. GABA is the body's endogenous form of benzodiazapam, an anti-anxiety chemical used in the manufacture of drugs such as Valum, Xanax and Clonopin. Serotonin has been called the 'great civilizing hormone.' It helps one sleep, prevents depression and anger, and improves impulse-control.

When the production of these hormones is inhibited due to the increased levels of Cortisol and Norepinepherine, one experiences diminished happiness and joy, becomes more anxious, and is more easily angered. Coupling these changes with the fact that one's impulse-control is restricted, the correlation between stress and intermittent releases of anger, becomes obvious.

Summarizing Anger Management
Let's summarize what we have learned about anger and its management thus far.

We have spent the last several sessions looking at the following aspects of anger:

1. Understanding the nature of anger.

2. Learning to look beneath our anger to gain an awareness and understanding of our underlying emotions.

3. Digging deeper -- beyond our painful emotions, to discover and examine, the unresolved injustice in our life.

4. Learning to use techniques that aid in the release of our negative emotions.

5. Letting go of the injustice, or offender, who was responsible for our wounded emotions, and the emotions themselves.

There is one more major factor in anger-managemet: correcting these underlying injustices without sinning. Remember the biblical admonition: *"Be angry but sin not?"*

Personal Application:
How can one employ anger (the motivation to correct injustice) without violating this command to "be angry, but sin not?"

_____

_____

Be angry, but Sin not!
This final aspect of anger management is critical. Since anger is a magnificent motivation: a passion to correct injustice and balance the accounts between myself and my abusers -- how can I do this without violating that dual command, to "Be angry, but sin not?" To answer this, allow me to draw from a Bible story in the book of Genesis. The story I am referring to is mankind's first reported conflict after Adam and Eve's fall.

As the biblical story unfolds, Cain was angry with his brother, Abel. They had grown up in the same household but had chosen different careers. Abel was a rancher, involved in animal husbandry. [The biblical record says *"Abel kept flocks."*] Cain had become a farmer, a horticulturist. [It is similarly recorded that *"Cain worked the soil"* (Genesis 4:2)].

At some point in time, both of these brothers brought an offering to their Creator, Yahweh. Abel brought *"some of the firstborn of his flock."* Cain brought *"some of the fruits of the soil"* (Genesis 4:3-4). Reading on we discover that: *"The Lord (God, Creator) looked with favor on Abel and his offering, but on Cain and his offering, he looked with disfavor. So Cain became very angry and his face was downcast.*

"*Then the Lord said to Cain, 'Why are you so angry? Why is your face so downcast? If you do what is right, will you not be accepted? But, if you do what is not right, sin is crouching at your door.* **It desires to have you, but you must master it**.*"* (Genesis 4:4-7, emphasis added). Cain didn't listen. He refused to change his ways or control his anger. In fact, he allowed his anger to grow until it controlled him. In his rage, Cain premeditated and carried out his brother's murder.

These few verses inscribed on an ancient scroll contain the essence of anger management. We have no idea what the original issue was between these brothers, but one thing we are pretty sure of: there must have been some past, unresolved issue between them. Why? Cain and Abel had both come to bring an offering to the Lord. At this point in biblical record, the only offering that had been instituted was the "sin-offering" (the offering of an innocent animal for the sins of man). This was the foreshadowing (or symbol of that future event): God's offering for man (a life for life, a soul for a soul), referred to in Genesis 3:21.

Cain and Abel must have experienced a major, albeit unrecorded, conflict. They had apparently "sinned" (or missed the mark) in their relationship. Both must have recognized that this since both brought an offering -- a sin offering. Abel followed the example and admonition of Yahweh, sacrificing an innocent animal as a symbol of the injury he had inflicted on one of God's children. Cain, on the other-hand, brought fruits of the ground.

Personal Application:
Cain was a farmer, so what was wrong with his sacrifice?

_____

_____

There is nothing wrong with fruit, nor with a fruit offering. In fact, the Bible gives specific instructions regarding the sacrifice of agricultural produce (i.e., the offerings of grain and meal). Such offerings, do not, however, meet the prescription given by God to man for a sin offering. Sin offerings required life for life, blood for blood.

Cain refused to comply with the directions God had given. He might have reasoned, "if I offer an animal sacrifice, I will have to acquire the animal from my brother!" Rather than humble himself, he proudly, and arrogantly decided to do his own thing -- present a sacrifice -- *his* own way. When his prideful act was rejected by Yahweh: when it failed to get him what he wanted, Cain became exceedingly *angry.* God warned Cain, but Cain failed to listen or master his anger. Instead, He allowed his anger to escalate into uncontrollable rage, that motivated him to murder his brother Abel.

Cain's *anger* (his motivation or passion to correct the injustice) was *exceedingly* strong. He certainly didn't lack in his desire to balance the account between Abel and himself. His deficiency lay, not in the level of desire to correct the injustice, but., in his unwillingness to use this motivation constructively.

Personal Application:
What exactly did Paul mean when he said, "be angry but sin not?

_____

Being angry and sinning not, as the Apostle Paul admonishes us in the New Testament, is like a warning sign -- similar to the warning God issued Cain. Paul was cautioning us to use our anger correctly. It takes strong internal counsel to rectify, or resolve, an injustice between ourselves and another person without missing the mark of relationship harmony. Hurting another person physically, spiritually, emotionally, intellectually, environmentally or socially is certainly missing that mark.

Personal Application
What then is the proper use of this motivation to correct injustice called anger?

_____

Successful Anger Management primarily involves self-correction. It may occasionally involve constructive, non-abusive correction of our children. But, it should *never, never* involve the correction of our spouse or partner. Remember, your spouse, your fiancee, your partner, is *not* your child, servant, slave or employee. He/She is your partner, your teammate, your compatriot and companion.

Scripture says:

BE ANGRY, BUT SIN NOT
USE YOUR ANGER POSITIVELY
CORRECT YOUR OWN BEHAVIOR
DO WHAT YOU KNOW IS RIGHT

Listen again to the admonition given Cain

"IF YOU DO WHAT IS RIGHT, YOU WILL BE ACCEPTED,
IF YOU DO WHAT IS WRONG, YOU WILL BE REJECTED,
SIN CROUCHES AT YOUR DOOR --
IT DESIRES TO HAVE YOU.
YOU MUST MASTER IT!"

None of us needs to practice the mastery of sin. Most of us are pretty adept at sinning, or missing the mark. What we all need to learn is how to . . .

Master The Use of Anger!
Make Anger work for you,
Make Anger your Ally . . .
Anger is a powerful force --
one of mankind's strongest motivations.
Learn to master it!
Learn to Use Anger for Good.
Never Allow Anger to Master You!

Reconciling Past Injustices

[Forgiveness: The Key to Healing Wounded Relationships]

What is forgiveness?
- It is a chosen behavioral pattern, a choice to release and let go of the injustice.
- It is a voluntary act to turn the emotional debt over to God as you know Him.
- It is the willingness to proclaim the offender's pardon and absolution at the appropriate time.
- It is giving up all resentment, bitterness and hostility toward the offender.

- **Why should we forgive?**
  - So that we, ourselves, can be forgiven (Matthew 6:12-15; Luke 6:37-39).
  - Because Christ has forgiven us (Ephesians 4:32).

- **How should we forgive?**
  - From our hearts (core, inner man, deep emotions) (Matthew 18:35).
  - Unconditionally. Not "if you forgive me"; but, "I forgive you regardless."

- **What if I refuse to forgive?**
  - We will not be forgiven (Luke 6: 37-39).
  - It gives the powers of darkness a "foothold" (or platform of operation) in our life.
    (2 Corinthians 2:10; Ephesians 4:26, 27).
  - It causes bitterness, which will cause you trouble and contaminate those you are in relationship with (Hebrews 12:15).

- **When should I forgive?**
  - Immediately, just as soon as you realize that you have been offended, or when the offender asks for forgiveness.

- **How often should I be willing to forgive?**
  - Repeatedly and endlessly (Matthew 18:21, 22).

- **Steps to Full Forgiveness**
  - Be open, sincere, and humble, willing to listen and learn from the other person.
  - Be prepared to take responsibility for your error, and do not expect an apology in return.

- Take the initiative -- go to the other person and seek reconciliation, specifically with words.
- Pardon the offender -- resolve never to bring up the offense in public or share it unnecessarily with others; and *never* hurt the other person.
- Let God's healing flow into the relationship wound -- forgiveness and healing is a continuing process, not an event.
- Pray for the offender's healing.
- Look for qualities of good in the one who offended you.

- **Evidence of Forgiveness**
  - The evidence of true forgiveness is our willingness and ability to 'give as before' the incident of injustice.
  - The evidence of our personal healing is our ability to openly relate to God without guilt.
  - The path to the cross -- the putting to death of our pride -- and humbly seeking God's forgiveness -- should be the most well-worn path in our life!

Motivational Management Action Plan
- Take time to review the dysfunctional methods you have used in the past, in an attempt to correct the real or imagined injustices in you and your partner's relationship:

- List the things in your relationship that *"really make you angry."*

_____

- Look beneath your anger, to discover those deep, personal, painful emotions you experience when these things happen?

_____

- What old injustices are you harboring, deep within your subconscious mind?

_____

- What steps have you taken, or are you willing to take, in the forgiveness process?

_____

_____

- What *personal* problems and behaviors have you become aware of, that need changed in yourself, whether your partner changes or not?

- What new behaviors are you willing to commit to as a result of this understanding of the motivation called *anger?*

- What were the original relationship goals that you and your partner established?

- What can you do *personally* to get your relationship back on track, headed to those goals?

GLOSSARY

Clone - a copy of [having another agree with us in all things]

Empowerment - to be given the power or ability to perform or act

Forgive - to "give as before" the injustice, to let go, to reconcile the relationship

Functionality - ability to function properly

Garnish - a legal proceeding attaching the ownership of something

Scenario - the story of, a visual or verbal recollection of an event

Yahweh - the Hebrew name for God, translated Jehovah in some English translations

KEY POINTS

- **The four basic principles involved in forgiveness**
  - letting go, yielding up, or releasing the injustice
  - absolving, or pardoning, the offender
  - declaring that the account, or injustice, is now reconciled, settled, or balanced
  - making a public declaration of the offender's pardon

- **Responsibilities in forgiveness:**
  - **Man** - letting go of the injustice and the offender (releasing them to God as we understand Him)
  - **God** - reconciling, or balancing the accounts between you and your offenders

- **Vengeance**
  - **Man's** - to get even or hurt the hurter
  - **God's** - to effect change, to correct the offender

- **Stress-management techniques**
  - take care of the easiest problems first
  - don't cluster changes
  - don't ignore problems
  - don't put yourself in situations that are, by nature, out-of-control

- **Anger-management summarized**
  - understand the nature and purpose of anger
  - look below your anger -- experience and understand your emotions
  - go beyond your painful emotions and reexamine the unresolved injustices in your life
  - learn and practice the principles of releasing your emotions, the act of injustice, and the responsible offender

- **Learn to Master your use of Anger -- it is a valuable tool -- make it your ally!**

CHAPTER 8
CONFLICT RESOLUTION SKILLS
vs.
DIRTY FIGHTING TECHNIQUES

Summary Review

In previous lessons we discovered the true nature of anger: that it is a God-given, magnificent motivation, bestowed upon man to aid him in correcting injustice and restoring equity. We learned that anger management has to do with the appropriate use of this motivation, its primarily use being for self-correction. We examined the meaning, the need, and the process of forgiveness.

At the close of the last chapter you were given a homework assignment, designed to help you accomplish four tasks:

1. To gain insight into your own relationship weaknesses,

2. To let go of the offenses of others perpetrated against you,

3. To release the offender to God, declaring his or her pardon and absolution, and

4. To take positive steps to redirect our own self, getting back on track toward our original relationship goals of harmony, happiness, and fulfillment.

Personal Application:

Reviewing your homework assignment, what did you learn?

_____

What commitment to change have you made, and what progress have you made along this journey?

_____

_____

_____

Do you think that you can learn how to live without conflict?_____

Conflict and Conflict Resolution

Conflict is inevitable. No two people will ever consistently see, hear, taste, touch, feel, perceive, think, believe, or process information the same. Moreover, opposites, in personality type, are naturally attracted to one another.

Personal Application:
Why do opposites tend to attract each other?_____

_____

Is this healthy, or should one seek out a partner who thinks, feels,

and believes as he/she does? _____

_____

The attraction between opposites is part of God's design. Opposites see in one another a part of life that they can never personally occupy. Opposites are, because of this, fascinated with one another. Both seem to know intuitively that the only way they can truly understand part of reality is through the other's eyes, ears, perceptions, etc. It is this intrigue: the desire to discover that which we cannot personally experience, that provides direction, purpose, spark and desire in a relationship.

At the same time, opposites do experience more conflict than those with greater personality similarities. The more similar two people are in personality, the greater ease in understanding each other. On the other hand, people of similar personality types, similar cultural and family histories, similar perceptions, similar beliefs, etc., more easily become bored with one another. There is little that is unknown, little to discover, and the desire to discover the unknown is one of the major mysteries of intimate relationships. Couples with different personality types are forever learning, yet never fully knowing, one another.

There is between those of differing personality types the desire to know, to understand, and to share with one another, their private world. This desire is more pronounced in significant relationships such as marriage partners. There is a desire to create a common world of knowledge, understanding and intimacy. The level of transparency, or "oneness," desired is rarely achieved but always anticipated, hoped for and expected. It is this desire for this absolute oneness, coupled with inadequate communication and conflict-resolution skills, that can result in manipulative, coercive, maladaptive, often abusive, and sometimes violent relationships.

Personal Application:
How can the desire for intimacy contribute to violence and abuse?

_____

_____

Couples often desire oneness, that deep level of intimacy and solidarity, so much they are willing to employ whatever techniques they think necessary to create this equitable solidarity -- the totality of a new entity called "family." If a couple's constructive, functional relationship skills are inadequate, a shared, strong sense of love, coupled with an intense desire for unity, can actually produce a potential for abuse and violence. A lack of communication and conflict-resolution skills creates barriers to unity. In their quest for oneness, skill impoverished lovers are committed to break down every barrier to achieve their expectations. It is this desire for solidarity and oneness that often births a process we call *dirty-fighting.*

Dirty-Fighting Techniques

Personal Application:
What are some of the ineffective relationship "skills" you are aware of, that are in reality, dirty-fighting techniques?

_____

_____

_____

Dirty-fighting techniques are maladaptive patterns of behavior, employed by persons with inadequate relationship skills, in an effort to effect intimacy. These dirty-fighting techniques are particularly ineffective knacks which usually ensure that the desired intimacy eludes those who rely on them.

As we review some of the more common dirty-fighting techniques, keep score on the chart provided on the next page. Review the descriptions of these dirty-fighting techniques and check those techniques that your and/or your partner tend to use during conflict-resolution attempts. Discover which techniques you use in your relationship, and which ones you *think* your partner uses.

183

Remember, however, **your task is to change *you,* not your partner.**

Dirty Fighting Techniques

Technique	Self	Partner	Other Techniques
Timing			
Escalation			
Brown-bagging			
Generalization			
Cross-complaining			
Minimizing			
Catastrophizing			
Asking why			
Blaming			
Pull rank			
Don't listen			
Don't talk			
List past injustices			
Depersonalize			
Dehumanize			
Mind-reading			
Fortune-telling			
Sarcasm			
Avoid responsibility			
Leave			
Reject compromise			
Play the martyr			
Using money			
Using children			
Use comparisons			
Giving advice			
Getting even			
Use terminal language			
Use inconsistency			
One-upmanship			
Use volume			
Use illness			
Embarrassment			
Crucify them			
Preempt them			
Use purposeful misinterpretation			

Technique	Description
Timing	Pick just the right time to begin an argument. Late in the evening, in the middle of the night; just before your partner has to leave for work; as friends knock on your door; during your partner's favorite TV program; or, after several drink. The general rule when using this technique is to seek a the time your partner least expects conflict, and is least likely to win an argument.
Escalation	Move quickly from the issue at hand, to questioning your partner's personality or motive. Continue on to question their relationship values. Question whether it's even worthwhile to stay together. Interpret your partner's weakness as evidence of their intentional bad-faith and verification of the impossibility of your ever enjoying happiness together.
Brown-Bagging	List as many problems as you can think of, in as much detail as possible, as quickly as possible. Never stick to the original issue. Throw in all of the past problems you can think of. If your partner can't recall the issue, so much the better.
Generalization	Use words like "always" and "never" (i.e., "You are always late," or "You never listen to me." Your partner knows that these generalizations are not true. When used, he/she will try to defend themselves rather than focus on the issue. This will insure a misunderstanding and eliminate the need to find a real solution.
Cross complaining	React quickly to any complaint your partner voices with a cross-complaint of your own. For example, "If you think that I spend too much on clothes, what about all the unnecessary tools you buy?" If you do this properly, you can balance complaint against complaint forever, thereby totally ignoring the original issue that begged for resolution.

Minimizing	Discount or downgrade the importance of any issue your partner brings up. For example, you might say, "So I used a little drugs. It's no big deal, nobody got hurt. You're just making a big deal of it because you're jealous." Never acknowledge the seriousness of any issue, or that it really needs to be resolved.
Catastrophizing	Exaggerate the importance of any issue you wish to win, with statements such as "If you really loved me, you would never have done that." "This proves that you really don't care." Or, "I can never trust you again." Never concede that an issue is not absolutely critical and in need of immediate resolution.
Asking why Questions	Why questions, i.e., "Why are you so late?" or "Why don't you clean up the mess?" imply that there is something basically wrong with your partner's judgment or that the problem exposes a basic character flaw. All other types of questions -- who, what, when, where, and how, are queries for more detail. In contrast, why questions make a person defend their personhood and forget the issue.
Blaming	Make it very clear to your partner that the problem is entirely their fault. Let them know that you are the innocent victim. Never admit that your behavior plays any part in the issue. Make sure your partner understands that he or she must change first, to save the relationship.
Pull rank	Never depend on the simple merits of your position. You might lose an argument. Pull rank by reminding your partner that you make more money, have a better education, more experience, are older, wiser or more popular. Use whatever it takes to enhance your status at your partner's expense.

Don't listen	If you listen, you run the risk of making your partner think that you value them or their opinion. Consider using back-talk, interrupt, call a friend while they're talking to you, or simply pretend to read or fall asleep. What ever you do, don't let them catch you paying attention to them.
Don't talk	Refusing to respond when they talk to you is a sure way to get their goat. Practice this technique so that you can catch everything they say to use against them later on, while making them think you are in another world. This technique is called the "violence of silence." With practice, you can become so adept, you will even be able to ignore their very presence.
List past injustices	Reciting every little injustice and inequity you have experienced in the relationship is a great morale builder. It will help you experience a renewed sense of self-righteousness. You can use this skill to justify almost any activity. For example, you might say: "Sure I bought a new car. So what? Look at all the new clothes you buy!"
Depersonalize	Never use your partner's first name, or terms of endearment. Labeling your partner with one or more negative titles such as: childish, neurotic, paranoid, stupid, insecure, jealous, sex-addict, bum, or alcoholic, can create the impression that they are completely worthless and totally to blame for all conflict.
Dehumanize	If depersonalizing doesn't work well enough, try dehumanizing your partner. Calling him/her a "lazy pig," "worm," "jackass," "mule-headed," or some other debasing, non-human title, will surely get them off track. They will probably forget about the original issue that needs solved.
Mind-reading	Declaring that you know the *real reason* your partner behaves in a certain fashion, will enable you to avoid debating the *real* issue. Saying "I know what you are *really* thinking," "I know where you're going," are other particularly effective schemes.

Fortune-telling	Predicting the future will usually save you the trouble of trying to resolve conflict. For example, saying, "You will never change, no matter what I do." Or, "you won't believe me, no matter what I say," are statements that can help you avoid dealing with the real issue without having to expend much effort.
Sarcasm	This a a great way to say something critical or demeaning without having to take any responsibility for it. If you can say, "Well, you're so smart" just right, you can imply that your partner is really stupid while denying that this was your intent.
Avoid responsibility	While not a very elegant tactic, saying "I don't remember" can bring most discussions to an abrupt halt. Using alcohol, drugs, or fatigue as an excuse is almost as successful. For example: saying "I must have been drunk," "high," or "tired out," are excellent ways to stop a discussion and prevent resolution.
Leave	Walk out of the room; leave home for a few days; or just go outside. Sometimes, just threatening to leave can accomplish the same thing without experiencing the inconvenience involved in actually leaving.
Reject compromise	Never, never back down. Why settle for a compromise when, with a little luck, you can really devastate your partner, perhaps even destroy the relationship? Stick with a win/lose, one-winner philosophy at all costs.
Play the martyr	If timed properly, playing the martyr card can totally disorient your opponent. Saying, "you're right dear, " I'm always wrong." Or, "I know, I *am* hopeless," can bring most conflict-resolution attempts to a dead stop.
Using money	Saying "If you made as much money as me," or "When you make as much as I do, you will deserve equal treatment as an equal," is an old, but very effective dirty-fighting trick, that will side track any attempt to resolve other issues.

Using children	Advising your partner, "If you spent more time with the kids, they would be doing better in school," or asking, "Do you want the kids to grow up like you?" can always be used -- unless you're so unfortunate as to have no children at all -- or perfect ones.
Use comparisons	Saying, "When you act like that you're just like your mother," or, "You are as stubborn as your father," is sure break up your partner's concentration, undermine their confidence, and deflect the argument from the original, relevant issue.
Giving advice	Give unsolicited advice. Telling your partner what to think, how to feel, how to act, and what to believe, while insisting that you are just trying to be helpful, can help you maintain a position of superiority while subserviating your partner.
Getting even	Never settle for a compromise. Never accept apologies. Hold grudges for as long as possible. You may need these unresolved complaints to win future arguments.
Use terminal language	Threaten to end your relationship. Perhaps you could even threaten to kill yourself, making sure that you let your partner know that if you do commit suicide, it will be all their fault since they make your life intolerable.
Use inconsistency	Keep changing your position. This is sure to keep your partner off balance. Try complaining that your partner never talks to you. Then, when they do talk, interrupt them or refuse to listen to what they say.
One-upmanship	Make your partner look bad by doing his/her duties before they can get to them, or try to do them better than they can. This will really demoralize him/her and demonstrate your superiority.
Use volume	Make your partner understand that "whoever is the loudest is always right." Then, make sure you win the prize. Shout, yell, scream, or curse. Do whatever it takes to win.

Use illness	Manipulate your partner into undertaking your tasks by pretending to sick. Convincing them you are too ill to even help yourself, let alone help them or the children, will help you avoid most conflict-resolution attempts.
Use embarrassment	Embarrass your partner or other person in public. Embarrass them in front of their friends and family whenever you get the chance. This technique will particularly demoralize them, often insuring that you get your own way.
Character Assassination	Move quickly from the issue at hand to questioning the other person's temperament, character and personality. Interpret the other person's shortcomings as evidence of a bad character, personality disorder or family traits.
Create Witnesses	Allege that others -- particularly family and friends -- share your opinion, and quote from them, as though you are representing them.
Crucify them	Keep your partner or other person "on the cross." Never express your forgiveness, and never accept their apology. If they tell you they were wrong, say, "that is obvious." If they say they're sorry, say, "you certainly are!"
Preempt them	Frequently remind your partner that their plans will never work out. Explain to them that their dreams and visions for life are wholly unrealistic, unworkable or both.
Intentionally misinterpret	Reframe everything you partner says. Take care to intentionally misinterpret and twist their intent and purpose. With practice this technique will make them think they're really stupid.
Volcanic Eruption	Erupt, blowing off steam using a string of name-calling, vulgarity, circular and incoherent speech. Be so forceful the other person retreats out of fear.

My Special Dirty Fighting Techniques.
The foregoing list is certainly not comprehensive. Take time to identify other styles of dirty-fighting that both, or either of you,

use. List these additional "skills" on the right side of the chart above, under "other techniques." Perhaps you have special dirty-fighting techniques you can share with us. After all, none of us should be deprived of such good "problem-solving" techniques!

_____

_____

_____

_____

_____

_____

Personal Application & Meditation Time:
Take a break, and while on break, reflect back on your partnership relationship. How many of these dirty-fighting techniques do you and your partner use when you experience conflict and attempt to resolve it?

_____

_____

How many conflicts have you and your partner ever solved using these dirty-fighting techniques?

_____

Have you tried anything else, or are these the only techniques you know, the only "conflict-resolution" tools you have?

_____

End Dirty-Fighting & Begin Conflict Resolution!
In an earlier lesson that focused on the skill of stopping abusive behaviors and setting new goals, we discussed the concept of repentance. You may recall that the word *repentance* means to "turn around and go in the opposite direction." You may recall, we demonstrated that no one can go in two directions at the same time. One cannot go in a direction opposite of the one they are traveling, until they quit going in that direction. To go in another direction, one must turn away from their present, or prior, goal and focus on a new one. Having turned around, faced in a different direction, one can no longer see their old, dysfunctional goal.

Commitment, Courage and Change
When we recognize that many of our old "problem-solving" techniques are actually "dirty-fighting" techniques; that these techniques serve to escalate, rather than resolve, conflict, it will

be easier for us muster up the courage to stop using them and embrace change. Effecting change in our behavior patterns does require courage, since our old behavioral patterns, however dysfunctional they might be, are comfortable. They are like a well worn shoe, very familiar, well practiced and an easy fit.

Personal Application:
Why, when we recognize the need for change, does change take so much courage and commitment to accomplish?

_____

_____

Any behavioral change, including new, improved conflict-resolution techniques, will feel unfamiliar and uncomfortable when we first experiment with them. Regardless of their viability, they are not instinctive but, take forethought to carry out. New behaviors always seem strange at first. They require practice for one to execute them with competence. When conflicts arise, we want to feel competent -- confident of the outcome. Thus, we tend to approach these situations by relying on our well-practiced skills. The result -- unless we practice our newly acquired skills -- will be to revert to the old, the familiar, and often inept, conflict-resolution efforts.

Personal Application:
How can one prevent slipping back, into the old familiar, abusive patterns?

_____

_____

Strong commitment and great courage are required during any skill development period. Developing any new skill requires much practice. Developing new skills to replace old ones, requires even more commitment, courage and practice. When developing a new, replacement skill, one must remain focused on their new goal, and avoid looking back at the old one. Looking back confuses our internal goal-seeking mechanisms, and results in our employment of our old, dysfunctional techniques.

The _commitment to change_ involves a great deal more than mere desire. Making a commitment to achieve something means that reaching our new goal is a personal imperative. It must be a consuming passion, not just an idle pastime. Reaching our goal for true intimacy needs to become a compulsory, mandated requisite of life, not just a wistful, unfulfilled dream.

Individuals who have experienced a significant amount of conflict in their relationship have often given up on their dream to achieve intimacy and oneness. They have often developed a misbelief that such intimacy and oneness is not even possible. To change, they must now battle against their own misbeliefs.

This requires *courage* to go against the grain, to violate one's own life-experience and foundational beliefs. It takes courage to behave differently and risk being misunderstood and maligned by those we love.

Personal Application:
What is the preeminent requirement in effecting behavioral change?

Taking personal responsibility to change one's own behavior, while family relationship dynamics seem to remain the same, is the essential, preeminent requisite to change. Your partner and other family members may not understand what you are trying to accomplish. Consequently, they may even try to sabotage your efforts. Changing one's personal behavior, particularly when others lack understanding and resist the change, requires substantial courage. You will especially need to have strong commitment and courage, if you seem to be the only one in the relationship working toward developing better conflict-resolution skills.

Personal Application:
If I am the only one working toward change -- isn't it hopeless?

It may at times seem hopeless. It is more difficult to accomplish any meaningful change in a relationship unless both parties are working together. However, it is not impossible, Significant change effected by one person in a relationship will effect change throughout one's entire family. The members of a family are bonded to one another. Because of this attachment bond, each person affects the way that the others act.

Change throughout the entire family system *must*, and will, occur if you are committed, courageous and patient. As you change. the old relationship dynamics once used in your relationship will no longer work. This will create a certain stress in your relationships -- stress that will motivate your spouse, children and others desiring to maintain a relationship with you, to effect change in their own lives, to retain their position in your life.

Personal Application:
Why is changing so difficult and sometimes painful?

_____

_____

It is imperative to remember that *change*, all change, results in some amount of internal stress (tension or pain). Skill-building is somewhat similar to bodybuilding. Every athlete understands the meaning of the old cliché, "No pain, No gain." Letting go of old, familiar patterns constitutes a loss, which may, to one's subconscious, seem like an injustice suffered. Practicing new skills, challenges one to behave in a fashion that is unfamiliar and uncomfortable, one in which they are initially uncomfortable and have no competence.

Within us is a process called homeostasis. Homeostasis is designed to keep us balanced and stable. Normally, this serves us well but, when we begin to change any pattern of behavior that has become a habit, own inner being fights against that change. Similarly, there is relational homeostasis working within any family system. Once again, it is designed to insure stability and security. Therefore, when one person in the family attempts to change something that all are involved in (i.e., communication and conflict-resolution techniques), the other family members will naturally resist. When this happens, it is important to remember, they are not intentionally being difficult. They are merely trying to maintain stability in the family system.

Conflict-Resolution:
The Alternative to Dirty-fighting
In comparison to the dirty-fighting techniques we reviewed earlier, we will now change our focus to look at an entirely new method of conflict-resolution. This method, called the "Ten Steps to Success," has a proven track record for effectively resolving conflicts. This technique helps partners avoid completely, engaging in the blame game and fault finding.

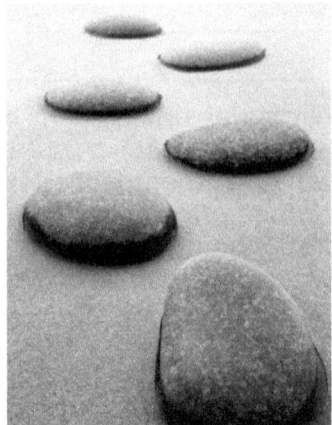

Relying on this method, there is never a need for one person be found to be found guilty and the other exonerated, to bring closure. It is not based on 'right vs. wrong.' The solutions reached by this method are designed to meet the needs and fulfill the desires of both parties. Yet, the 'rules' or precepts this method is based on never results in rigid, legalistic, unchangeable solutions.

For a relationship to be healthy, setting rules in concrete needs to be avoided. Developing and enforcing rigid, legalistic relational rules is merely a setup, leading to future conflict. Life is dynamic. It continues to change over time as one ages, and as circumstances change. What works today will probably not work five, or ten, years from now. These changes require alterations, or adjustments, in one's personal, vocational and relational rules and boundaries. Making appropriate change as conditions warrant, go a long way to insure conflict-resolution success.

CONFLICT RESOLUTION
Ten Steps to Success

❶ **Set an Appointment** - When a conflict first arises, emotions usually run high. Setting an appointment with the other person to talk the issue over, allows your partner or other person sufficient time to get in touch with his/her position, thoughts, emotions and beliefs surrounding the issue.

Pushing for immediate conflict-resolution is an almost sure way to effect conflict-escalation rather than conflict-resolution. Thus, trying to immediately engaging the other person when one wants to resolve an issue, or settle a problem, is included among the dirty-fighting techniques. It normally results in escalating emotions and triggering an argument.

❷ **Employ Dialogue vs. Discussion** - Make sure that you keep the appointment. When you meet, begin your conflict resolution efforts by engaging in dialogue. Dialogue is *not* the same as discussion. Discussing an issue always revolves around the question: 'who was right and who was wrong?' Discussing an issue is about finding "fault" and assigning "blame."

Dialogue, on the other hand, is not in-and-of-itself problem-solving. However, dialogue it is a prerequisite for all successful problem-solving. Dialogue involves investing the time to clearly understand each other's position, so that problem-solving efforts can remain focused and be productive.

Dialogue involves a process of communication called "active listening." Active listening includes learning to listen to one's partner so carefully that you can feed back the essence of their position with minimal distortion, concise enough that the other person *feels* understood. Dialogue also includes a recognition of what the speaker is conveying non-verbally -- in their facial expressions and gestures -- which may be different from that expressed in their words.

Dialogue requires the participants to employ focused *listening*, not than the more common habit of just *hearing* what the other is saying, while simultaneously rehearsing one's own position. That is merely waiting for the other person to pause long enough for one to interject their position. When we do this, we rarely hear, and almost never understand, what the other is saying.

❸ **Take a Break** - Carrying dialogue to the point of understanding requires patience, Dialogue consumes a lot of emotional energy, particularly in times of conflict. Emotional pressure is apt to surface during times of dialogue. Pushing on toward conflict resolution at that point, usually intensifies emotions, often resulting in an argument. Take breaks, as needed, during your dialogue to allow your emotions to settle.

Whether or not you needed to take a break, or breaks during your dialogue, when your dialogue is complete, and each of you have a thorough understanding the other person's position, you will need to take a break. This break should be long enough for your own, and your partner's, emotions to settle down, restoring calm. It must also be long enough to give you time to reflect over the information gleaned through dialogue, and sufficient to gain insight.

❹ **Seek Insight** - During this break, take time individually -- apart from one another -- to review your dialogue. Take time to identify the *real,* core issue or issues?

_____

_____

What are the principal differences between your own and your partner's, or other person's, position?

_____

_____

What did *you* do, or not do, that contributed to the misunderstanding?

_____

What, if anything, did you to prevent the problem from being resolved?

_____

_____

What triggers or cues did you, or your partner, exhibit?

_____

_____

❺ **Share Your Insight** - After your break, compare what each of you thinks are the real issues. If there is more than one, come to an agreement on an agenda for considering each one -- one at a time.

1) _____

2) _____

3) _____

Confess what each of you did that contributed to the misunderstanding or problem.

1) _____

2) _____

3) _____

4) _____

Make a list of the ineffective problem-solving efforts (or dirty-fighting techniques) either of you have used in the past, in an effort to solve similar problems, that have not worked.

1) _____

2) _____

3) _____

4) _____

❻ **Implement Forgiveness** - Forgive each other for using those old dirty-fighting techniques. Remember, to forgive, means first of all, to let-go. Enter a covenant with each other (preferably a written contract) that you will commit to no longer using those methods.

1) _____

2) _____

You needn't judge each other or try to assign fault or blame for using dirty-fighting techniques. Just recognize that since they don't work, they don't work. To continue using these ineffective techniques will only cause new problems and pain.

As part of the process of forgiveness and change, implement the instruction given in James 5:16: *"Confess your faults one to another, and pray for each other, so that you (your relationship) may be healed. The prayer of a righteous person is powerful and effective."*

❼ **Brainstorm Together** - Take time to list together of all the possible alternative techniques each of you might try, in seeking a solution to the present issue. Be willing to list anything that either suggests.

1) _____

2) _____

3) _____

4) _____

5) _____

After your imaginations are exhausted, consider the pros and cons of each alternative. Rate the practicality of each on a scale from zero to ten, with zero being completely impractical and ten being the most practical.

❽ **Take a Test-Flight** - Select one, or a combination of alternative techniques from your list. Identify each person's responsibility in trying these alternative techniques.

1) _____

2) _____

Agree to test them for a specified period of time:

_____

Now, set an appointment to meet at the end of this test-flight period to review your success.

❾ **Quality Control** - Meet at the appointed time and place to review the outcome of your test-flight. Check out the progress each of you has made in completing his or her assignment. Remember, this meeting is for the purpose of "quality-control," not to assign fault or blame. Check out the quality of your new skills. If they are working well, agree to try them for a longer period of time. Fine-tune them as necessary. Replace any components that seemed not to work. Keep trying and making fine-tuning adjustments until you find a set of skills that work well.

Using the following Conflict-resolution Assignment form, practice these ten steps to success until they become well oiled.

Assignment
[Conflict-Resolution Practice]

Log your conflict-resolution practice for the week and indicate how far through the process you make it

Conflict No. 1	Conflict No. 2	Conflict No. 3
Describe the Event:	Describe the Event:	Describe the Event:
Did you take a time out?	Did you take a time out?	Did you take a time out?
Did you set an appointment?	Did you set an appointment?	Did you set an appointment?
Did you keep the appointment?	Did you keep the appointment?	Did you keep the appointment?
Did you successfully dialogue?	Did you successfully dialogue?	Did you successfully dialogue?
Did you remember to take a break after your dialogue?	Did you remember to take a break after your dialogue?	Did you remember to take a break after your dialogue?
In reflecting, what did	In reflecting, what did	In reflecting, what did

Conflict No. 1	Conflict No. 2	Conflict No. 3
you think the real issue was?	you think the real issue was?	you think the real issue was?
What did your partner think the real issue was?	What did your partner think the real issue was?	What did your partner think the real issue was?
What was your contribution to the problem?	What was your contribution to the problem?	What was your contribution to the problem?
Did you ask forgiveness?	Did you ask forgiveness?	Did you ask forgiveness?
What dysfunctional methods had you used unsuccessfully to resolve this and similar issues?	What dysfunctional methods had you used unsuccessfully to resolve this and similar issues?	What dysfunctional methods had you used unsuccessfully to resolve this and similar issues?
Are you willing to stop using these unsuccessful methods?	Are you willing to stop using these unsuccessful methods?	Are you willing to stop using these unsuccessful methods?
What alternative did you and your partner agree to try?	What alternative did you and your partner agree to try?	What alternative did you and your partner agree to try?

Conflict No. 1	Conflict No. 2	Conflict No. 3
How long did you agree to try this before a review?	How long did you agree to try this before a review?	How long did you agree to try this before a review?
How will you reward success?	How will you reward success?	How will you reward success?

Personal Application Assignment:
Practice this ten-step conflict-resolution skill program over the next month, or as long as it takes until you feel conformable using it, beginning to become competent in its use. Initially, use the preceding conflict-resolution log. Using this format, will help you work through any conflict as far as you can. Don't let your emotions escalate to the point of inflicting additional emotional pain in your partner. If you get stuck, take a break and try again. If you seem to reach an impasse in your efforts, take the issue to a qualified counselor of your choice, and ask him/her to help you work through the remaining steps.

⑩ **Reward Success** - Reward each other for each successful conflict resolution. Even if full solution was not achieved, affirm each other for the positive efforts made in movement toward an agreed solution. Keep your eye on the goal and reward success. Never, never reward bad behavior with "make-up" gifts and never punish one another.

Summary:
If you will take a few minutes to review these conflict-resolution steps, you will notice that they never result in "final" closure. This is because the proper resolution for a specific conflict today, may not work for the same, or a similar type, of conflict tomorrow or next year. Circumstances and situations change. We are not static, unchangeable statutes. We are dynamic, living beings, whose lives continue to change from the moment of birth to the moment of death.

Good conflict-resolution skills must take this fact into account and be flexible enough to change with the times, the growth of individual family members, and other changes within one's family

-- changes such as illnesses, disabilities, changed work schedules, etc. Also, take note that at no time is there ever a determination of who is right and who wrong. No assignment of fault or blame is ever made. The focus is on finding solutions relationship problems, developing conflict-resolution behavioral patterns that work, and developing, or restoring relationship oneness and intimacy.

This ten step conflict-resolution technique allows for trial and error, without failure.

Remember, no genuine effort to find a solution is *ever* *wrong* since the entire process is experimental -- looking for workable solutions and developing personhood-honoring skills.

GLOSSARY

Coercive - to restrain or constrain by force, to force someone into a certain action

Dialogue - sharing or exchanging views, opinions, or perspectives in order to enhance or improve both parties understanding

Imperative - absolutely necessary, compelling and/or urgent

Insight - to gain an understanding of one's own inner nature, self-talk, and motivation

Knacks - a trick, a clever, underhanded way to do something

KEY POINTS

- **Dirty-fighting Techniques**
  Review the various dirty-fighting techniques to see which ones you have been using and which ones you believe have been used against you.

- **Keys to Lifestyle Modification**
  (changing long-established behavior patterns)
  - **Commitment**
  - **Courage**
  - **Change**

- **Maintain Goal Focus**
  (keep focused on new, desired behavior -- NOT the old one you wish to stop)

- **Skill-practice**
  Practice the new, desired skill until it becomes a habit (something you do without thinking). This usually requires consistent behavior for a period of two to six weeks.

- **Ten Steps to Successful Conflict-resolution**
  - **Set an Appointment**
  - **Use Dialogue vs. Discussion**
  - **Take a Break when needed**
  - **Seek Insight during breaks**
  - **Share Your Insight with Partner**
  - **Practice Forgiveness**
  - **Brainstorm for alternative methods**
  - **Take a Test-flight**
  - **Quality Control and Adjustments**
  - **Reward Success**

BIBLIOGRAPHY

A Course in Miracles, (1976), Foundation for Inner Peace, CA

Augsburger, D (1979), **Anger and Assertiveness in Pastoral Care,** Fortress Press, PA

Backus, W (1985), **Telling the Truth to Troubled People,** Bethany House, MN

Backus, W & Chapian, M (1980), **Telling Yourself the Truth,** Bethany Fellowship, MN

Backus, W (1991), **Telling Each Other the Truth,** Bethany House Publishers, MN

Backus, W & Backus, C (1990), **What Did I Do Wrong? What Can I Do Now?** Bethany House Publishers, MN

Backus, W (1987), **Finding the Freedom of Self-Control,** Bethany House Publishers, MN

Backus, W & Backus, C (1988), **Untwisting Twisted Relationships,** Bethany House Publishers, MN

Backus, W & Chapian, M (1984), **Why I do What I Don't Want to Do,** Bethany House, MN

Bass, E & Davis, L (1988), **The Courage to Heal,** Harper and Row, NY

Beck, A (1988), **Love Is Never Enough,** Harper and Row, NY

Bell, C (September, 1986), **Family Violence,** *Journal of the American Medical Association*

Berenson, D (Spring, 1990), **A systematic view of spirituality: God and Twelve-Step Programs, as resources in family therapy,** *Journal for Strategic and Systematic Therapies,* Vol. 9, No. 1

Bilodeau, L (1992), **The Anger Workbook,** CompCare Publishers, MN

Black, C (1982), **It Will Never Happen To Me,** MAC, CO

Bloomfield, H & Felder, L (1983), **Making Peace With Your Parents,** Random House, NY

Bobgan, M & Bobgan, D (1977), **The Psychological Way/ The Spiritual Way,** Bethany House, MN

Bowen, M (1978), **Family Therapy in Clinical Practice,** Jason Aronson, NY

Bowker, L (1983), **Beating Wife Beating,** Lexington Books, MA

Bradshaw, J (1988), **Bradshaw on: The Family,** Health Communications, FL

Bradshaw, J (1990), **Homecoming: Reclaiming and Championing Your Inner Child,** Bantam Books, NY

Bradshaw, J (1988), **Healing the Shame that Binds You,** Health Communications, FL

Brinegar, J (1992), **Breaking Free from Domestic Violence,** CompCare Publishers, MN

Brown, B (1977), **Stress and the Art of Biofeedback,** Bantam Books, NY

Buber, M (1958), **I and Thou,** (Second Edition), Charles Scribners Sons, NY

Burwick, R (1981), **Anger: Defusing the Bomb,** Tyndale House, IL

Buzawa, C & Buzawa, E (1996), **Domestic Violence: The Criminal Justice Response, 2nd. Ed.,** Sage Publications, CA

Cahill, A (1981), **Aggression Revisited: The Value of Anger in therapy and Other Close Relationships,** *Adolescent Psychiatry 9*

Carlson, D (1987), **Counseling and Self-Esteem,** Word, TX

Carpenter, E (June, 1985), **Traumatic Bonding and the Battered Wife,** *Psychology Today*

Carter, L & Minrith, F (1993), **The Anger Workbook,** Thomas Nelson Publishers, TN

Cermak, T (1986), **Diagnosing and Treating Co-Dependency: A Guide for Professionals Who Work with Chemical Dependents, Their Spouses and Children,** Johnson Institute, MN

Cosgrove, M (1987), **Counseling for Anger,** Word, TX

Crabb, LJ (1987), **Effective Biblical Counseling,** Zondervan, MI

Dobash, R & Dobash, RE (1979), **Violence Against Wives,** The Free Press, NY

Druck, K & Simmons, J (1985), **The Secrets Men Keep,** Doubleday, NY

Elgin, S (1995), **You Can't Say That to Me: Stopping the Pain of Verbal Abuse -- An 8-Step Program,** John Wiley & Sons, NY

Ellis, A (1977), **Anger: How to Live With and Without It,** Citadel Press, NJ

Ellis, A & Grieger, R (1977), **Handbook of Rational-Emotive Therapy,** Springer-Verlag, NY

Este's, C (1992), **Women who run with the Wolves,** Ballantine Books, NY

Evans, P (1993), **Verbal Abuse: Survivors Speak Out,** Bob Adams, Inc., MA

Evans, P (1992), **The Verbally Abusive Relationship: How to Recognize it and How to Respond,** Bob Adams, Inc., MA

Fabry, JB (1980), **The Pursuit of Meaning,** Harper and Row, NY

Finkelhor, D; Hotaling, GT & Yllo, K (1988), **Stopping Family Violence: Research Priorities for the Coming Decade,** Sage Publications, CA

Flores, B (1990), **Chiquita's Cocoon,** Pepper Vine, CA

Fortune, M (1981), **The Church and Domestic Violence,**

Theology, News and Notes, Fuller Theological Seminary

Forward, S & Buck, C (1979), **Betrayal of Innocence: Incest and Its Devastation,** Penguin Books, NY

Fossum, M & Mason, M (1986), **Facing Shame: Familles in Recovery,** WW Norton, NY

Frankl, V (1963), **Man's Search for Meaning,** Pocket Books, NY

Frankl, V (1975), **The Unconscious God,** Simon & Schuster, NY

Frankl, V (1978), **The Unheard Cry for Meaning,** Touchstone Books/Simon & Schuster, NY

Friel, J & Friel, L (1988), **Adult Children: The Secrets of Dysfunctional Families,** Health Communications, FL

Frost, R (1963), **Selected Poems of Robert Frost,** (introduction by Robert Graves), Holt, Rinehart & Winston, NY

Gelles, RJ & Cornell, C (1985), **Intimate Violence in Families, 2nd. Ed.,** Sage Publications, CA

Gelles, RJ (1974), **The Violent Home: A Study of Physical Aggression between Husbands and Wives,** Sage Publications, CA

Gelles, RJ (1987), **Family Violence,** Sage Publications, CA

Gelles, RJ & Loseke, D (1993), **Current Controversies On Family Violence,** Sage Publications, CA

Glasser, W (1975), **Reality Therapy,** Harper and Row, NY

Goldstein, A; Keller, H & Erne', D (1985), **Changing the Abusive Parent,** Research Press, IL

Gruen, A (1986), **The Betrayal of Self: The fear of autonomy in men & women,** Grove Press, NY

Harris, B (1993), **Spiritual Awakenings: A guidebook for experiencers,** Stage 3 Books, MD

Hart, A (1986), **Adrenaline & Stress,** Word, TX

Hazelden (1989), **Setting Boundaries: A Moment to reflect** (booklet), Hazelden, MN

Helfer, R & Kempe, C (1974), **The Battered Child,** University of Chicago Press, IL

Hunter, RS & Kilstrom, N (1979), **Breaking the Cycle in Abusive Families,** *American Journal of Psychiatry 136*

Jones, A (1980), **Women Who Kill,** Rinehart & Winston, NY

Jourard, S (1968), **Disclosing Man to Himself,** Van Nostrand, NY

Justice, B & Justice R (1976), **The Abusing Family,** Human Sciences Press, NY

Katherine, A (1991), **Boundaries: Where you end and I begin,** Parkside Publishing, IL

Kellogg, T & Harrison, M (1990), M: **Broken Toys Broken Dreams: Understanding Codependency, Compulsive Behavior and Family,** BRAT, MA

Kubler-Ross, E (1969), **On Death and Dying,** Macmillian, NY

Larson, B (1974), **The One and Only You,** Word, TX

Lerner, H (1985), **The Dance of Anger,** Harper and Row, NY

Levinson, DJ (1978), **The Season's of a Man's Life,** Ballantine, NY

Lowen, A (1985), **Narcissism: Denial of the true self,** Collier/Macmillion, NY

Lowry, R & Meyers, R (1987), **Conflict Management and Counseling,** Word, TX

Malone, TP & Malone, PT (1987), **The Art of Intimacy,** Prentice Hall, NY

Martin, G (1987), **Counseling for Family Violence and Abuse,** Word, TX

Maslow, A (1961), **Toward a Psychology of Being,** Van Nostrand, NY

Masterson, JF (1988), **The Search for the Real Self: Unmasking the personality disorders of our age,** Free Press/MacMillian, NY

May, R (1953), **Man's Search for Himself,** W.W. Norton & Co, NY

McMinn, M (1987), **Cognitive Therapy Techniques in Christian Counseling,** Word, TX

McMinn, M (1988), **Your Hidden Half: Blending Your Public and Private Self,** Baker Books, MI

McMinn, M (1990), **Dealing With Desires You Can't Control,** NavPress, CO

Meichenbaum, D (1977), **Cognitive-Behavior Modification,** Plenum Press, NY

Miller, A (1990), **The Untouched Key,** Random House, NY

Minuchin, S (1974), **Families and Family Therapy,** Harvard University Press, MA

Narramore, S (1984), **No Condemnation,** Zondervan, MI

Neidig, P & Friedman, D (1984), **Spouse Abuse: A Treatment Program for Couples,** Research Press, IL

Noller, P (1980), **Misunderstandings in Marital Communication: A Study of Couples' Nonverbal Communication,** Journal of Marriage and Family Counseling 39

Nouwen, H (1973), **The Wounded Healer,** Doubleday, NY

Novaco, R (1978), **Anger and Coping with Stress: Cognitive-behavioral Interventions,** Cognitive Behavior Therapy, Plenum, NY

Rekers, G (1987), **Counseling Families,** Word, TX

Rogers, C (1961), **On Becoming A Person,** Houghton Mifflin, NY

Rosenbaum, A & O'Leary, KD (February, 1981), **Marital Violence,** Journal of Consulting and Clinical Psychology

Rossenbaum, A (June, 1986), **Of Men, Macho, and Marital**

Violence, *Journal of Family Violence 1*

Roy, M ed, (1977), **Battered Women: A Psychosociological Study of Domestic Violence,** Van Nostrand Reinhold, NY

Satir, V (1987), **Conjoint Family Therapy,** Science and Behavior Books, CA

Satir, V (1972), **Peoplemaking,** Science and Behavior Books, CA

Scarf, M (1987), **Intimate Partners: Patterns in Love & Marriage,** Random House, NY

Seamands, D (1981), **Healing for Damaged Emotions,** Victor Books, IL

Seamands, D (1982), **Healing of Memories,** Fleming H. Revell, NJ

Sonkin, D & Durphy, M (1985), **Learning to Live without Violence,** Volcano Press, CA

Stacey, A & Shupe, A, **The Family Secret,** Beacon, MA

Steinmetz, SK (1977), **The Cycle of Violence: assertive, Aggressive, and Abusive Family Interaction,** Praeger, NY

Steinmetz, SK, (1978), **The Battered Husband Syndrome,** *Victimology 2, Nos 3 & 4*

Stoop, D (1982), **Self-talk: Key to Personal Growth,** Fleming H. Revell, NJ

Straus, Gelles & Steinmetz (1980), **Behind Closed Doors: Violence in the American Family,** Anchor, NY

Task Force on the Family, (1985), **Report of the Survey of Family Development Concerns of Pastors,** National Association of Evangelicals, IL

Taverns, C (1982), **Anger: The Misunderstood Emotion,** Simon and Schuster, NY

Tournier, P (1967), **To Understand Each Other,** John Knob Press, GA

Tournier, P (1983), **The Healing of Persons,** Harder and Row, NY

VanCleave, S; Byrd, W & Revell, K (1987), **Counseling for Substance Abuse and Addictions,** Word, TX

Vitz, P (1977), **Psychology as Religion: The Cult of Self-Worship,** Eerdmans, MI

Walker, L (1984), **The Battered Woman Syndrome,** Springer, NY

Walters, R (1987), **Counseling for Problems of Self-Control,** Word, TX

Walters, R (1981), **Anger: Yours, Mine and What to Do About It,** Zondervan, MI

Warren, N (1985), **Make Anger Your Ally,** Doubleday, NY

Wegsheider, S (1981), **Another Chance: Hope and health for the alcoholic family,** Scientific and Behavior Books, CA

Weinbold, BK & Weinbold, JB (1989), **Breaking Free of the**

Co-dependency Trap, Stillpoint, NH

Welter, P (1987), **Counseling and the Search for Meaning,** Word, TX

Whitfield, CL (1987), **Healing the Child Within: Discovery and Recovery for adult children of dysfunctional families,** Health Communications, FL

Whitfield, CL (1985), **Spirituality in Recovery,** Perrin & Treggett, NJ

Whitfield, CL (1991), **Co-dependence: Healing the human condition,** Health Communications, FL

Whitfield, CL (1993), **Boundaries and Relationships: Knowing, Protecting and Enjoying the self,** Health Communications, FL

Wilber, K (1978), **No Boundary,** Shambhala, CO

Wills-Brandon, C (1990), **Learning to Say No: Establishing Healthy Boundaries,** Health Communications, FL

Wilson, E (1983), **The Undivided Self: Bringing your Whole Life in Line with God's Will,** InterVarsity, IL

Wilson, E (1985), **The Discovered Self: The Search for Self-Acceptance,** InterVarsity, IL

Wilson, S (1987), **Counseling Adult Children of Alcoholics,** Word, TX

Woititz, J (1983), **Adult Children of Alcoholics,** Health Communications, FL

Wright, HN (1986), **Self-talk, Imagery, and Prayer in Counseling,** Word, TX

Wright, HN (1984), **Making Peace With Your Past,** Fleming H. Revell, NJ

Yancey, P (1977), **Where is God When It Hurts?** Zondervan, MI

Other Books for Your Enjoyment

If you enjoyed, and profited from, this book, Dr. Potter and Paula have written a number of other books you may find of interest. Most focus on family relationship issues and spiritual growth. They include the Save Our Families series, the Living Sober - Living Free series, and a new series titled, Mysteries of the Bible.

The "SAVE OUR FAMILIES" SERIES

The "Save Our Families" Series provides life-changing answers to age-old problems that destroy families and individual's lives. Each volume facilitates a growing personal relationship between the student and Jesus Christ, through a personal application of the Scriptures. Each Volume addresses specific barriers that stand in the way of oneness with our Creator, providing faith-based Scriptural keys for overcoming these barriers.

Mastery Over Anger, is a Biblically based manual to help those with anger problems gain the skills to effectively control their anger and use it appropriately -- to resolve problems rather than create them and/or hurt the ones they love. In eight information-packed lessons, the author provides keys to stop angry outbursts, to get below your anger into the underlying emotions, to examine the injustices that gave rise to such emotions, and how to release the emotions and resolve old injustices. The volume closes with a comparison of ineffective "dirty-fighting" techniques and a proven Ten Step approach to effective conflict resolution.

Assertiveness, Individuation & Autonomy, answers questions such as: Have you ever said yes to someone's request when you really didn't want to? Do you feel like other's owe you certain help, favors, love, etc., or that you owe them? Do you ever feel like your partner is trying to control you? Do you feel trapped, possessed and dominated? Do you ever feel like your being treated like a piece of property in your relationships, rather than a unique child of God? Do you ever tell a "white lie" or just not answer to avoid conflicts? If you answered yes to any of these questions, you need this nine lesson book that can change your life. God desires relationship *with* us, not ownership *of* us. And, our relationship with God should serve as the model for all our relationships.

Conquering Codependency - Do you sometimes feel like "you're walking on egg shells" around those you love to avoid arguments? Do your partner's emotions (i.e., anger, sadness, depression, etc.), affect your emotional state? Do you sometimes have trouble knowing where your boundaries end and another person's begin? Are there areas of your life where you lack healthy personal boundaries, or perhaps have such rigid boundaries that you easily offend others? Do you need help understanding and developing healthy personal boundaries and limits? Do you tend to focus on other's negative characteristics rather than their positive characteristics? And, do you have trouble surrendering your life to God? If so, this volume is for you.

Arrested Development & Personality Disorders - If you have ever been accused of having a Dr. Jekyll/ Mr. Hyde personality, or live with someone who does, this volume is for you. This volume examines the process of personality development, demonstrating how one's personality can become bent, predisposing that person to various personality disorders and an inability to develop healthy bonding. It reveals the underlying cause of this distortion -- the loss of love -- and the resulting manifestations of rejection and rebellion that give rise to addictions, compulsions and other life-controlling problems. This volume also lays the groundwork for answering some of life's most important questions: Who am I? What is the meaning of my life experience? What is my purpose? Where am I going? And, How do I get there? It closes with a powerful exercise that, when used, can help break any compulsivity or addiction.

Healing Inner-Child Wounds -. This volume begins where life begins -- in the womb -- at the beginning of human development. Each chapter begins with a reexamination of one of life's developmental stages, the developmental tasks of that stage, factors that can sabotage our developmental progress, and aberrant adult behavior that often results from our failure to successfully traverse this path; and closes with exercises and meditations that help us bring closure to that stage of life and move on toward maturity. Topics include: overcoming rejection and abandonment issues, developing trust, hope, love and faith, defusing obstinate-defiant thoughts and behavior, giving up magical thinking and restoring creativity and, developing self-awareness and competence. Ideal for use in inner- child workshops.

Toxic Shame and the Journey Out - This volume employs the powerful twelve step approach to break one of life's most controlling, most destructive problems -- toxic shame. Below every addiction, compulsivity and/or other life-controlling problems, including toxic shame. Shame, unlike guilt, is not about what I have done, but rather, about who I am. Shamed to the very core, we develop a negative self-image and corresponding poor self-worth. Then, because each of us needs affirmation and approval -- if only from ourselves -- we act-out our negative self-concept thereby exacerbating our shame. Toxic Shame and the Journey Out, provides a gentle, faith-based approach to recovery.

Growing Beyond Our Genetics: Adolescence & Beyond - Adolescence is troubling, mystifying period of development commencing around thirteen and continuing until one reaches about twenty-six. It is a season of life during which we leave childhood and journey toward maturity, a time during which we acquire many life-management skills: some positive and some rather dysfunctional. A stretch during which we may experience positive parental guidance or profound abuse, either of which will impact every significant relationship we develop as well as our own parenting skills. Have you ever wondered about the effect of your genetics on your personhood -- your aptitudes, attitudes, characteristics, and behavior?

This volume examines the life-span development tasks and pitfalls of adolescence; the effect of genetics vs. environment; the development and healing of Misogynists (men who hate and fear women), Misandrists (women who hate and fear men), Misogamists (persons who hate and fear marriage). Moving on from this beginning, we scrutinize the impact of our family lineage on the development of misbeliefs, life-commandments and disorders, employing a Family Time Line and Family Genogram to illustrate the impact of genetics. The volume closes with a study on the "new birth" which literally means to be **re-gened**, and demonstrates through Biblical and scientific reference the enormity of change possible if we just believe.

Affair-Proof Your Marriage and Escape Relationship Bondage - Marriage is the most anticipated, most sought after, and often the least rewarding event in life. It was designed -- by the creator -- to create oneness and provide companionship and intimacy. However, married life on planet earth is full of change and change produces stress -- stress that can bind a couple together or drive them apart, depending on the couple's level of bonding and their ability to communicate and solve conflicts. Unresolved they lead to disenchantment, separation and divorce. In this volume, you will be introduced to God's model for the human family ("Made in His image"). Then we will expose the greatest divorce and affair-prevention tool available: Human Bonding. You will be given the 12-steps of human bonding, and bonding repair techniques. Following this lead in are dynamic lessons on couple communication, conflict-resolution, and approaches to intimacy enhancement .

The "Living Sober - Living Free" Series

Counseling Addicts & Offenders: A Guide to Criminal Justice Counseling - If you have ever been involved in counseling addicts, perpetrators of domestic violence and other criminal justice offenders, you are all too familiar with the judicial marry-go-round of arrest, conviction, incarceration, release, arrest, etc., etc. Why, knowing the outcome, do addicts and offenders keep on doing the same things? Because, as you will learn in this volume, they process information distinctly different from other people. Their cognitive and affective thought processes are different; their foundational beliefs and values are different; and alas, their goals and motivations are different. Attempting to correct their problem through behavior modification therapy is much like trying to cover a melanoma with a Band-Aid. But, through this volume, you will learn to understand the mental processes of the addict and offender; discover new therapeutic techniques and modalities that have proven successful; and learn how to select the most appropriate treatment setting.

Substances of Abuse - A detailed psychoactive substance identification and symptom guide. If you are a substance abuse and addiction counselor, a member of the judiciary, a concerned parent, or a student pursuing certification in substance abuse and addiction counseling, you will find this guide invaluable.

The "Mysteries of the Bible" Series

Mysteries of the Bible - Adam to Abram: The Primeval Era - the first volume in this series - was released in January, 2009. In this volume you will find answers to those questions that seemingly remain unanswered: questions about the fallen angels, the Nephilim, the giants and more. The authors take you into the original languages of the Bible to help you understand seemingly incomprehensible mysteries.

ABOUT THE AUTHORS

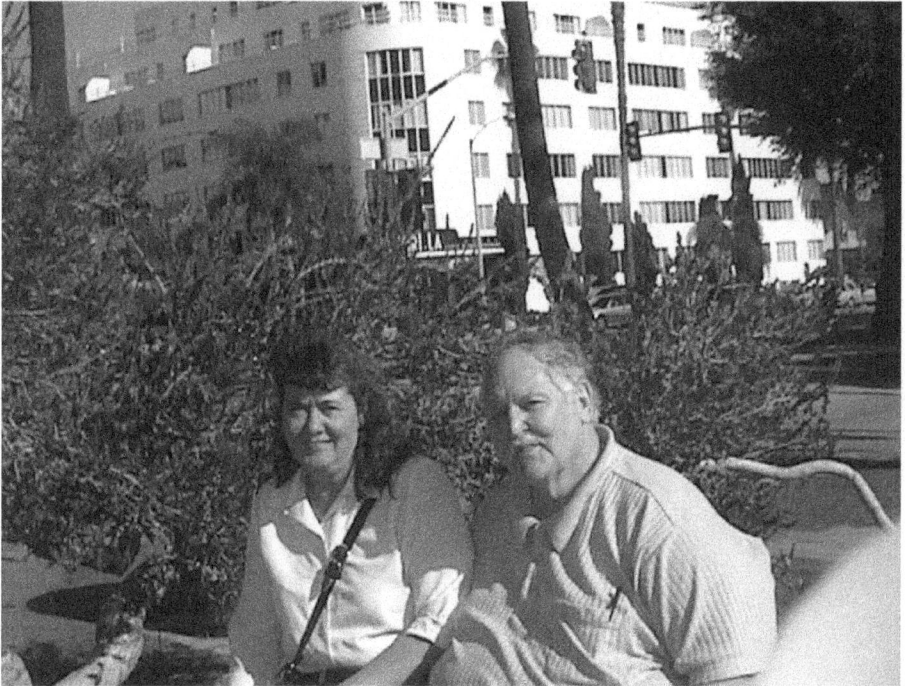

Dr. James V. Potter and Paula M. Potter, husband and wife, are Christian authors, counselors, educators and ordained ministers. Dr. Potter and Paula make their home in Northern California. Prior to moving to California, Dr., and Mrs. Potter served with the Family Ministries School of the University of the Nations, Youth With A Mission (YWAM) in Hawaii; as Associate Pastors with The New Covenant Churches and the Gospel of Salvation Ministries, Hawaii. They founded the Hawaii Family Care Centers, a network of community-based Christian Counseling Centers in Hawaii, Agape Family Services, Alliance Recovery Services, AFS Family Skills Institute and AFS Publishing, in California.

Since retiring from private clinical practice, Dr. And Paula Potter have founded Advocare Ministries and its divisions, Advocare Publishing, dedicated to publishing Christ-centered counseling resources and self-help guides; and Advocare Family Skills Institute, to carry on the training and equipping of Christian Counselors.

Dr. And Paula Potter are Certified Christian Marriage and Family Therapists, Certified Clinical Pastoral Counselors, Certified Addictions Counselors, and Certified Domestic Violence

Specialists. Dr. Potter was awarded the prestigious Fellow Award by the American College of Forensic Counselors, and is a Diplomate under the American Association of Christian Therapists.

Dr. Potter is a member of the World Association for Online Education and is listed in Who's Who in America, Who's Who in the World, Who's Who in Religion, Who's Who in Education, in the International Biographical Centre, and In Men of Achievement.

Dr. James Potter, and Paula Potter, MA, can be reached at:

Jubilee Enterprises
P.O. Box 994114
Redding, California 96099
www.advocareministries.com

www.ingramcontent.com/pod-product-compliance
Lightning Source LLC
Chambersburg PA
CBHW031249090426
42742CB00007B/381